MW00443887

"In this remarkable book, Donna Phelan shows women how to create their own prosperity by learning how to manage money, invest their savings, repair their credit, learn to budget and take control of their future. The strategies are new, refreshing and easy to apply to one's life. Indeed, this is the best book written on money for women, by an expert woman in the field."

—Mark Waldman, Author of *Words Can Change Your Brain*, Executive MBA Faculty, Loyola Marymount University

"Donna's book supports women as they take control of their own financial and retirement planning."

—Rochelle Schneider, Attorney at Law, Executive MBA, RJS Legal & Business Consulting

"This book provides 'aha' moments. Donna does an excellent job of getting the point across through a powerful story in a simple, understandable format. She allows readers to 'peek behind the curtain' of investing and financial planning, and address our unique challenges as women."

—Debra Hoffman, Independent Agent, Medicare Health Plans, Life, Health and Long Term Care

"This book shows women how to create prosperity by learning about money in simple terms. It makes the complicated world of finance clear and understandable and emphasizes how important it is for women to become knowledgeable and comfortable around their money. This is a subject from which women are often excluded. This book inspires women to create income and shows them the importance of being responsible for their own security in retirement. Donna Phelan provides creative ideas for saving and increasing income while empowering women by showing them they have choices."

—Linda Gauthier, Fine Art by Linda

"I can highly recommend Donna Phelan's *Women, Money & Prosperity* because it provides excellent advice on how to select successful investments. The book is recommended, entertaining reading for women whose longer life spans counsel an independent guidance of money management. Although Donna's personal life experiences and financial advice will resonate with independent women, her book is for men also because managing money should be a productive exercise for everyone."

—Rear Admiral Herb Bridge, USNR (ret)

"Phelan's encouraging voice and simple, action-oriented tasks help make retirement planning not only attainable, but also fun and fulfilling. Thinking about several income streams encourages creativity, which is a word not usually associated with financial planning—very refreshing!"

—Katie Frankle, Director of Project Management

"This book explains the unique challenges that put women behind in retirement saving without blame or guilt, and gives them simple steps to get ahead."

—Erica L. McCain, LUTCF, Safe Money Specialist, and Owner/ President of McCain & Associates of Ohio, LLC

"This book is an easy how-to for women and their finances. This is what women have been waiting for to help them take charge and answer their questions."

—Melissa Roe, AIF(R), CIMA(R), Managing Director, Divisional Manager, Nuveen Investments

"This book offers great financial strategies that empower women to create and maintain several income streams."

—Jacqueline Howe, Entrepreneur

For Ronald White,
Wishing you success and
prosperity in all your endeavors!
Donna M. Phelan

WOMEN, MONEY
&
PROSPERITY

A Sister's Perspective on
How to Retire Well

DONNA M. PHELAN, MBA

ISBN hardcover: 978-1-939758-33-0
ISBN eBook: 978-1-939758-34-7

For information contact:
800-375-2580
info@donnamphelan.com

In Chapter 12, I reference from *Unveiling the Retirement Myth: Advanced Retirement Planning Based on Market History*, written by Jim C. Otar, CFP, CMT, BASc, MEng. In his book, he provides detailed charts and concepts, which I draw upon and then use to build my own advice. Thank you, Jim, for your sage advice.

This book is lovingly dedicated
to my mother,
Mae Elizabeth Cully Phelan,
an incomparable role model,
who always encouraged me to be my best,
and who personified excellence
and joie-de-vivre.

Contents

Contents

In Appreciation

I would like to express my deep appreciation to the many people who encouraged and supported me in this passionate writing project.

Special thanks to my editors at Business Ghost: Michael Levin, CEO, whose excellence and vision helped to crystallize the important concepts of this book. Thanks to Bree Barton, CCO, an outstanding professional writer and a delight to work with, who helped to personalize the book and develop a readable storyline. Thanks to Sara Stratton, COO, also a professional writer, who was extremely gracious, helpful and organized in the completion of this project.

I would like to thank Jim C. Otar, CFP, CMT, BASc, MEng, brilliant author of *Unveiling the Retirement Myth: Advanced Retirement Planning Based on Market*

History, for his important work on retirement portfolio withdrawal rates, on which many of the assumptions in Chapter 12 are based.

I would like to thank my business partner, Malinda S. Difley, MBA, CFP™, whose wisdom, insights and financial acumen constantly enhance my perspective.

Thanks to my web designer, Cayley Vos, of Net-paths.net, whose uncanny understanding of social media greatly enriched this project.

Thanks also to Marsha Friedman of EMSI Public Relations and her highly professional team for their excellent work on my behalf.

Special thanks to Dr. Christopher A. Manning, PhD, Professor of Finance, Investments and Real Estate at Loyola Marymount University, Los Angeles, for his insightful contributions regarding the capital and real estate markets.

Thanks to Mark Waldman, Faculty, Executive MBA Program, College of Business, Loyola Mary-mount University, Los Angeles, author of twelve books, including *Words Can Change Your Brain*, for his role as mentor, and for the generous introductions he made on my behalf.

To RADM Herb Bridge (ret), many thanks for his constant encouragement, high intelligence, and experienced voice in always encouraging me to persevere and finish the book.

In Appreciation

Thanks to Jane Donnelly Schmitt, an important leader in the economic, political, and educational advancement of women.

I would especially like to thank my sister, Sharon C. Rosenberg, who always encouraged, supported, and believed in me throughout the long process of writing this book. She is a treasure of strength, generosity, and kindness. I thank you from the bottom of my heart. And loving thanks to my sisters, Carol Sullivan Lauraitis and Lois Sullivan-Taylor, for their warm-hearted support.

A special note of gratitude to my mother, Mae E. Phelan, my greatest inspiration, and her sister, Alice Lawlor—the two sisters I admire most. And my deepest appreciation and thanks to all my family and friends—truly too many to name—who were the constant, collective wind in my sails.

Retirement Planning for Women: An Oxymoron?

I knew from the moment Joan walked into my office that she had come to tell me a dirty little secret.

Joan had called the week before to set up our first meeting to start planning her retirement. I knew from the information she'd given me over the phone that she had worked in banquet sales for a large, grand, local hotel for nineteen years—a job she liked and was successful at and had every intention of keeping until she retired in twelve more years at sixty-five. She had two fine, grown children and a relationship with her ex-husband that was amicable; they'd worked well together even after their divorce to put the kids through college and had split the cost of the educations more or less fifty/fifty. Her mother was still living, and she visited her at least twice a week in the upscale nursing home where she now resided.

Joan herself lived in a two-bedroom condo with a five-year-old Yorkie named Ming, drove a Lexus, swam a mile every morning at her neighborhood health club, and walked into my office wearing a smart business suit, polished and practical heels, pearl earrings, and a warm smile that gave me every reason to believe she was very, very good at her job in the hospitality industry. She looked the very picture of a competent, energetic businesswoman who had everything going for her.

But I saw the hint of panic hidden behind the nice clothes, the professional smile, and the vellum business card she offered me.

What gave her away?

She was a fifty-three-year-old woman who had come to me for help to *start* planning for her retirement.

Unfortunately, Joan's situation isn't an uncommon one in today's society. As a senior investment professional, with one of the largest and most respected investment firms, I have spent eighteen years lecturing about, writing about, and working one-on-one with people to help them manage their investments and plan for their retirements. During this time, I've advised men and women, young and old, professionals and entrepreneurs, corporate executives and small business owners, within almost every income bracket.

But it is the almost countless mid-life women, like Joan, who have walked into my office over the years, with whom I seem to make an almost immediate connection. This is likely because, as a woman myself, I understand the real-world financial challenges that are unique to women. I know the marketplace handicaps, I've encountered the cultural obstacles, I'm in on the dirty little secret: that is, however successful, hard-working, diligent, and practical we have been as individuals, there are, simply, financial disadvantages inherent in being female.

However many cracks there might now be in that proverbial glass ceiling, down here at ground level not much has changed for the average working woman. Preparing for retirement as a woman in the early years of the twenty-first century is an exercise that would stress any woman out, which is why most of us put it off to the point of panic—or beyond. The tight, lingering handclasp that Joan and I shared was simply a soundless way of acknowledging that we understood each other: I *got* her financial fears; she didn't have to hide anything from me.

What was more—I kept my gaze level and my own smile reassuring as I led Joan to a seat near my desk—there were tactics that she could employ to reverse her shaky post-employment plans. I was going to let her in on a secret of my own: It didn't have to be too late for her to create an abundant retirement for herself.

In this book, as with Joan, I will be taking a different approach, one that illustrates how women need to establish income for life. It's not a question of getting to the goose egg or the golden pot; it's the fact that women need several stackable income streams *(See page 93)*. They need income for life, and they need to always be earning, even in retirement.

If there is a feminist anthem playing in your head right now, you can turn it off. I'm not here to talk politics: I'm here to talk money. My only purpose here is to help women like Joan find security for their retirement years. Whether it be a single woman in her twenties who wants to start planning early or a grandmother of three realizing her savings will run out only a few years into her retirement, women face unique challenges in their financial planning and therefore need unique advice to help them through it.

Is retirement planning for women an oxymoron?

I don't think so, and now I'd love to show you why.

Chapter 1

Designing Your Future

This book was written for women just like you, who want to retire but are afraid they won't be able to. It is for women who feel a low-level fear that they are getting close to retirement and wonder if they will have enough saved. Maybe you are already in retirement, either by choice or because of premature downsizing, and are questioning what you should do next.

You know who you are—you are the mothers, the daughters, the sisters, the wives, and the grandmothers who have taken care of everyone else, and now know you need to take care of yourself and your own retirement but don't know how. You want to retire with financial security and peace of mind, *knowing* that you have enough saved. This book will show you how.

WOMEN, MONEY & PROSPERITY

Women, Money & Prosperity gives you simple, actionable steps to get you from where you are today—less than sure—to where you want to be—financially secure.

In general, women have it tougher than men in the workplace throughout their careers. As of the U.S. Census in 2010, women who worked full time still only earned 77 percent of men's salaries—a median income for women coming in at $36,931 compared to $47,715 brought in by men.[1]

Although the wage-earning gap has narrowed over the second half of the twentieth century, the disparity still accumulates over time, resulting in the average woman losing $431,000 over the course of a forty-year working career.[2]

Not only do women tend to earn less than their male counterparts, they lose years from their careers to have and raise children, they face glass ceilings men can't imagine, and they have the constant struggle of being true to their natures or "one of the boys." So why should it come as a surprise that women have it tougher than men when it comes to their retirement, too?

This is a book about a challenging prospect, retirement, especially in today's uncertain, seemingly no-growth economic climate. For a generation of seventy-seven million Baby Boomers, however, the subject can't be avoided any longer. And of those seventy-seven million, more than half are women who will be facing significantly different financial challenges than their male colleagues.

But don't women and men enter retirement in tandem? How can a woman's experience be that much different?

The answer, sadly, is that women earn less, often spend more time and money on child care and elder care, and usually outlive men, meaning they live longer in retirement than men and with fewer resources. In fact, on average, women tend to live five to six years longer than men. By age eighty-five, there are roughly six women to every four men, and the gap only increases as we age.[3]

Here's a harsh statistic: As of 2009, statistics for the elderly show that women are twice as likely as men to be living below the poverty level—13 percent in contrast to 7 percent of men.[4]

That's an astounding number. But how do so many women end up in such a financially perilous situation? There are a variety of reasons, stemming not only from a woman's financial situation but also from the lifestyles many women lead, whether those lifestyles come from their own choosing or are forced upon them by circumstance. In order to illustrate the specific challenges that women face, let's briefly look at the stories of four women who embody the most common situations in which women approaching retirement age will find themselves: widowed; divorced; married with children; and never married, with a full-on career.

FOUR SISTERS

Despite being very close, the Strong sisters could not have chosen four more different lifestyles. Oldest sister Wanda, for example, found herself widowed at age fifty-six with only her husband's small life insurance policy helping to pay her big mortgage. With the average age of widowhood being in the mid-fifties, Wanda is in the same unenviable state as many other women her age—unprepared.[5]

It's very typical that women in their mid-fifties, in particular widows, do not have access to all of the benefits they might need. Even Social Security makes them wait to collect unless they have young children, and many times, if a husband has died unexpectedly, he may not have made preparations to ensure that his widow receives his benefits—which is exactly what happened to Wanda.

Moreover, Wanda has two kids in college while at the same time shouldering the responsibility of caring for her husband's elderly parents. Not well enough to live on their own any longer but unable to afford assisted living, they moved in with Wanda shortly before her husband's death in the hope of spending their last few years with their only son and his family.

As a result of this situation, Wanda is the perfect example of the "sandwich generation"—women who are sacrificing many of their wage-earning years to taking care of both children and parents. In many cases, as with Wanda, a woman can suddenly find herself as not only the sole caretaker but also the only wage earner in the family, forcing her to figure out resources and a new game plan on her own.

Wanda's sister, Debbie, on the other hand, is a divorced artist who supports herself as a freelance contractor. At first glance, it may seem like she is in a better position than Wanda—after all, Debbie didn't suddenly find herself without the resources and benefits she had been relying on to support her in her "golden years." After her divorce, she received a substantial settlement from her former husband and still had time to plan and save. Additionally, she lacks the extra financial responsibilities of children or elderly parents. Debbie, it initially seems, should have no problems with retirement.

However, the interesting statistic about women and divorce is that, while men often remarry shortly after separating from a spouse, women are much more likely to remain single.[6] What does that mean from a financial standpoint? Well, it means that a divorced woman has much higher per capita living expenses than someone who is divorced but remarries and shares expenses with another person.

In the case of Debbie, she is the sole proprietor of a business she owns, so she is responsible for her own benefits as well. Unfortunately, the stress and hard work of her career have adversely affected her health, which means she can't work as often and, as a result, has little money coming in and no health insurance. Sadly, many women find themselves in a similar situation. They are completely self-dependent and don't have the backup resources to help them with things such as disability insurance on top of the day-to-day expenses of simply living alone.

At the opposite end of the spectrum is Marilyn, who is a happily married stay-at-home mom whose CEO husband has all of the perks and benefits that go along with his position—the rich compensation plan, a big 401(k), a pension, and an insurance retirement plan that is typical with high-powered CEOs. As his wife, Marilyn has access to all of those benefits, but none of it is in her name and she has no real funds of her own.

As with Debbie, Marilyn initially appears to be in a very good situation. However, as I just mentioned, none of this is in Marilyn's name. What if, like Wanda, she finds herself widowed or, like Debbie, divorced?

Thanks to her husband's great benefits, Marilyn has been able to save and pay off the mortgage on their large home, but her three young children are all in private school, and although college is still a distant thought, Marilyn knows how expensive tuition can be. She also realizes how unpredictable life is—should anything happen to her husband, Marilyn is now realizing she could find herself in a very tenuous position. How, then, can she begin planning for possibilities that may be beyond her control?

Finally, the youngest Strong sister, Sara, is the single girl in the bunch. She has a great job with a large corporation, her own condo, and an active social life filled with nights out with friends at trendy restaurants and clubs. At first glance, she seems footloose and fancy-free. It's been a longstanding joke in the Strong family that she is continually looking for Prince Charming to come and sweep her off her feet, but all of the jibes are good-natured. Sara loves her single life and has no desire to marry anytime soon. In general, she appears to have a great set-up.

Nonetheless, as we've seen with the other Strong women, not all is as it seems.

Sara has a good job with a financially sound company, but, unlike her male counterparts, she isn't in line for any promotions and doesn't receive as many of the perks. She has her own condo, but she lives alone, so, like Debbie, she shoulders all of the expenses. Sure, she has good benefits through her job, but she also has a higher mortgage and more financial burdens that come from her single lifestyle.

Like her male counterparts, Sara is also expected to

entertain her work colleagues for dinner and cocktail parties throughout the year. However, unlike those colleagues, Sara doesn't have a spouse to share both the financial cost and preparation time needed for hosting these types of important work-related social events. As with everything else, Sara is on her own.

I recently read an interesting statistic: as of 2010, 43 percent of Americans over the age of eighteen are classified as single by the U.S. Census Bureau, and more than half of those are women.[7] I found that number surprisingly high, but it can't be denied that more and more women are choosing to get married later in life or to not marry at all. Unfortunately, as a result, they may find themselves in a difficult financial position as they prepare for retirement.

FROM CHALLENGES TO OPPORTUNITIES

The situations the Strong sisters find themselves in exemplify many of the problems facing retiring women today—lower wages, wage-earning years lost to caregiving, fewer promotions and therefore smaller pension plans, and living arrangements that leave them with greater financial burdens—but those challenges are simply chances to turn a bad situation into an advantage.

In the corporate world, women earn less and, as a result, have smaller retirement savings. They also see their wage-earning years reduced by childbearing and rearing—the time off also adversely affecting their promotions and perks. As a result, their financial portfolio at the time of their retirement is much thinner than that of their male counterparts. Yet women will live longer and be more affected by inflation over the years, so they see their savings reduced more seriously due to longevity. As with Wanda, women simply tend to live longer than their spouses.

As a woman, I am more likely to live alone by virtue of divorce or widowhood, forced to shoulder financial burdens on my own. I am also more likely to be the primary provider and caretaker for children and aging parents, draining my reserves of time, money, and opportunity. Because of this, I will live longer in retirement with fewer retirement resources.

In general, women start late on the retirement planning process and, as a result, are so overwhelmed by the concept that they can barely consider planning a viable retirement. They put their heads in the sand, which will only make the problem worse. However, because more traditional paths can be closed to them, women should be more willing to take the chance and look at non-traditional ways of creating retirement planning. Most important, they must establish vehicles that will allow them to continue earning into their retirement years so that their finances aren't dependent on savings or pensions that may dry up more quickly than expected.

Women need to make a viable plan and continue earning throughout retirement.

With this book, I would like to accomplish three very important goals: providing *awareness*, offering *hope*, and outlining *strategies*.

AWARENESS

There are numerous challenges facing women nearing retirement age, but many are realizing the dangers too late, which is why awareness of the situation needs to be raised. It is not simply a matter of "everyone goes into retirement at the same time, so what's the difference?" Women face certain challenges that are unique to women. As I mentioned earlier, it's not solely about a disparity in pay. It's a domino effect that begins with a difference in lifestyle and cascades down to a difference in pay, perks, and promotions.

Ultimately, the most important thing to recognize is that women are in their own demographic group when it comes to retirement. As such, they may have unspoken fears about retirement planning—fears that no one is addressing. Some people believe that "retirement planning for women" is an oxymoron, since most women feel they will never be able to retire. The truth is, because women aren't aware, they don't know what they are doing right or wrong, or even that they should be doing things differently at all.

That needs to change.

HOPE

It may not seem like it at the moment, but there is a way for women to create a strong retirement plan that will allow them to do well in their "golden years." However, currently many women lack hope, which saps them of the courage needed to move forward *now*. It causes them to feel fearful or depressed when they start to look at the realities facing them in the coming years.

Feelings like that threaten to immobilize them, but this book will provide women with the hope they need to take control of their lives on a step-by-step basis. It will help them look at their financial future logically and give them the tools to take back their power, tools such as controlling their credit, learning about their finances, and creating SISTERS clubs—which I'll discuss at length in later chapters—where they can commiserate with other women and maybe even strategize on methods for creating stackable income streams that could fund them for the rest of their lives.

But it all begins with hope.

STRATEGY

Finally, and most important, this book will offer women real life strategies for figuring out financial security throughout their retirement years.

First and foremost, women must change their mindset. They need to stop viewing retirement as a single event and start seeing it as an ongoing lifestyle that requires an ongoing income. In order to do this, they need to be earning for themselves no matter how old they are. They can no longer just retire and hope their money lasts; instead, they need to begin following through on strategies that will create the required income—investing in dividend stocks or annuities, for example, or starting up a home-based business.

Consider Sara Blakely, the woman who created Spanx. Blakely was recently featured in the March 26, 2012, issue of *Forbes* as the youngest female self-made billionaire in the world.[8] It all began with a simple concept back in 2000—taking a pair of control-top pantyhose, eliminating the pantyhose, and using the remainder as a kind of mini-girdle. The idea took off, going from a small home-based business to a $1 billion corporation. Now every woman in America knows what Spanx are.

And it all started with a woman who turned her one simple idea into a home-based business.

Obviously, not every woman needs to come up with a billion-dollar idea in order to survive retirement, but the success of Spanx is a great example of what can happen when a person thinks outside the box of traditional financial planning methods. If you don't think you have enough money to start that business or build those annuities, why not consider downsizing or looking into nontraditional living situations, such as finding a roommate? All you have to do is get a little creative and open your mind to fresh ideas.

Sure, you can put aside ten dollars a month at 6 percent for the next thirty years, but for many women it's already too late in the game for that. They need strategies that will work sooner rather than later, and no one has told them that they have enough time, power, and resources—especially if they combine their strengths with other women—to create the retirement funding that will last them for years to come.

The time to start doing that, however, is *now*.

THE STARTING POINT

As I mentioned above, women need to think of alternative strategies for funding their retirement, and a big part of that is redirecting their mindset. They need to understand that the necessity of earning an income doesn't stop at sixty-five, at least not for women. Women must create several stackable income sources for life and recognize that they have the power within them to maintain these strategies.

But where does it all start? At times it may seem as though there is too much to learn, too much planning to do. How, you might be wondering, do you begin?

Well, picking up this book is a great start. Over the next several chapters, I'll discuss not only the specific challenges and fears women are facing as they near retirement but also outline a seven-step plan to help create the income women need in order to flourish in retirement.

Although there are plenty of other books out there about how to navigate the tricky waters of financial planning for retirement, this book is the only one specifically designed for women like you—those concerned about the future and how they can better prepare themselves.

Over the years, I have worked with a variety of women and spent a great deal of time studying the statistical analyses. More important, however, I have seen those statistics manifest in my life. It's brought me some pretty incredible realizations; witnessing the data substantiated so close to home was a sobering insight.

So how can you avoid becoming one of those statistics?

By taking a significantly different route in planning your retirement.

With years of experience on both sides of the desk— as a financial advisor and as a woman trying to save for retirement—I am uniquely qualified to help design a retirement plan specifically for women, addressing their needs and concerns better than any other program currently out there. So forget about waiting for Prince Charming to come along and pay your bills. Instead, invest your efforts in yourself and start planning to make those retirement years truly golden.

REFERENCES:

1 Glynn, Sarah Jane, and Audrey Powers. "The Top 10 Facts About the Wage Gap: Women are Still Earning Less Than Men Across the Board." Center for American Progress, April 16, 2012. http://www.americanprogress.org/issues/2012/04/wage_gap_facts.html.

2 Ibid.

3 Kirkwood, Thomas. "Why Women Live Longer." *Scientific American*, October 21, 2010. http://www.scientificamerican.com/article.cfm?id=why-women-live-longer.

4 "Time Trends in Poverty for Older Americans Between 2001–2009," Employee Benefit Research Institute. April 2012, Vol. 33, No. 4. http://www.ebri.org/publications/notes/index.cfm?fa=notesDisp&content_id=5046.

5 Kreider, Rose M. and Jason M. Fields, 2001. *Number, Timing, and Duration of Marriages and Divorces:* Fall 1996. Current Population Reports, P70-80. U.S. Census Bureau, Washington, DC.

6 U.S. Census Bureau. (2006). American Community Survey: 2006 (No. S1201): Marital Status. As cited in Bradbury, T. N., & Karney, B. R. (2010). Intimate Relationships. W. W. Norton & Company.

7 Petty, Linda. "Single? You're not alone." *CNN Living,* August 19, 2010. http://articles.cnn.com/2010-08-19/living/single.in.america_1_single-fathers-single-mothers-single-parents?_s=PM:LIVING.

8 *Forbes Billionaires,* March 26, 2012. http://www.forbes.com/profile/sara-blakely/.

Chapter 2

Moving Beyond the Anxiety

If women face an entirely different set of challenges when retiring, it makes sense that the fears driving them would also be very different from those of their male counterparts. While men are typically more financially secure at the time of their retirement, often with pension plans in place, larger 401(k)s, and greater amounts of money from years of working safely saved, women with less firm retirement plans worry about finding themselves out of money just when they need it the most—to provide for the years when they would be considered beyond earning age. In fact, in general, women are entering retirement with a much greater degree of anxiety than their male counterparts.[1]

Wanda Strong worries about becoming a burden to her children. Debbie is concerned that she will one day soon find herself unable to work and be forced to exhaust her little savings just to survive. Marilyn wonders what would happen should she find herself suddenly single—and without a financial plan—after years of being married. Sara considers what she will have to show for her years of hard work—and lack of promotions—once she retires.

As those Baby Boomers rapidly approach retirement age, more and more women are discovering that they are not nearly as secure as they had hoped to be at this time in their lives. And yet, few have offered an answer to their retirement planning problems.

Other retirement planning books gear you toward save, save, save, and hopefully you'll have enough saved by the time you get to retirement. I say: let's take a different approach. You need to be *constantly earning income*; otherwise, it's too easy to give into the variety of fears plaguing women about how to fund their golden years.

In general, expenses are increasing. Eighty-seven percent of women surveyed in 2009 worried that their health care costs would grow faster than their retirement income, while 83 percent believed their overall cost of living would increase beyond their retirement means.[2] Sadly, those fears are not unfounded. Health care alone is rising by 7 percent a year.[3] And in 2010–2011, college tuition increased an average of 4.5 percent at private colleges and 7.9 percent at public universities.[4] The historical rate of increase in college tuition is approximately 6 per-cent—significantly higher than that of general inflation. It goes without saying that these rates of increase are also substantially higher than the average increase in an American worker's personal income each year.

In such an economic climate, it's understandable to be worried. The trick, however, is not allowing that fear to overwhelm you or cause you to slip into poor finan-cial and personal habits.

A PICTURE OF FEAR

What do you do when you get nervous about money? Let me know if this sounds familiar: a gripping concern in the pit of your stomach—the bills are coming due and there is not enough money to pay them. It feels like a fist is clenching your gut and refuses to move.

At first you ignore it, but it nags at you peripherally. Finally, you try to sit down and sort through the bills, but that only raises your fear level. You sigh and push the papers around. Then you clean them up and reshuf-fle them. No relief. Deciding you need some advice, you turn on the TV to the financial channel. They are using words you don't understand. Unfortunately, none of their "guidance" helps.

You turn off the TV and look for something to eat, starting off with carrots and celery. Nevertheless, it isn't long before you put crunchy peanut butter on the celery.

Now fortified by food, you make another run at the bills. Still no good. You then reach for the cheese and crackers, which is still technically health food.

You sit down to balance your checkbook again, to see if you can't coax it into a little more cooperation, but it holds steadfast. The cheese and crackers turn into ice cream.

Before you know it, you're becoming dismayed and distracted as the fear creeps up from your stomach and clutches your throat. You can't breathe. You start to wish you actually smoked, just to give yourself some way of calming down.

Next thing you know, you are on the sofa with an alcoholic drink, staring blankly into space. You are immobilized—the fear has won.

A QUIET FEAR

In my years of financial advising, one of the many things I have noticed in my female clients is their quiet fear. They feel it at the end of every month when they don't have enough to pay their bills. It's the fear of not only running out of money but also of being a bad woman.

From the time we are small children, women are taught to be pleasant, to smile, to be sugar and spice and everything nice. As a result, we learn not to make a scene or complain. Unfortunately, this attitude becomes a real hindrance when we are faced with financial difficulties. Instead of speaking up, asking questions, or taking a more proactive stance, women often try to convince themselves and others that everything will be fine, even quietly sedating themselves because they can't find a solution—turning to alcohol, tranquilizers, food, shopping, and a variety of other coping strategies that will only worsen their situation.

This captures, frankly, what women don't talk about—that because we earn less yet have the same or even more financial obligations than men, we can get overwhelmed. Even worse, no one has taught us the solutions that will help us rectify the situation. You have to either earn more or spend less, and if you have a pile of bills waiting to be paid, spending less isn't an option.

However, earning more can be a tough prospect. As women, we have found the glass ceiling, and although it is slowly improving, we keep banging our heads up against it. So what do you do if you don't have the answer? You become inundated and fearful but keep those fears to yourself.

And sometimes the answers are just as daunting as the problems. One option that I'll discuss later in this book is striking out on your own with a business, but that carries with it a whole new set of worries. Again, as women, we are not often taught about business matters. Although attitudes are changing, when the generation of Baby Boomers was in college, women were never encouraged to pursue business; instead we were guided into liberal arts. As a result, we don't have mentors in the business world for younger women who may want to pursue that course.

Before getting into the business world, I actually worked in the jewelry industry trying to start my own jewelry design company. When I first started out, I flew by the seat of my pants and made all the rookie mistakes—underpricing my goods, failing to make the right contacts, and not keeping proper track of my books. It took a sales representative at one of the major jewelry retailers telling me that I was undercutting myself before I realized that I needed to strengthen my business acumen if I wanted my company to be successful. In order to get to that point, however, I had to come to terms with my fears and move past them.

Most women instinctively know they don't have enough saved. They don't have a strategy for rectifying that, and they feel like it's too late for them. That's why they go into quiet despair. They don't talk about it. They anesthetize themselves in one way or another— how else can you live with so much fear? Because they don't have financial literacy—a basic understanding of their own finances—they don't know what to do about it. They end up depressed and thinking, "This will never end. This is how it's always going to be." That is the mass consciousness of women—average, middle-class women. Women just like you.

However, there may be a way beyond that fear if you are willing to face it down and take some action.

FACING THE FEAR

Everyone has been afraid at least once in their lives and more than likely over money issues. Such fear can take many disguises: fear of making decisions, fear of making a mistake, fear of looking foolish or stupid, fear of the unknown, fear of not being good enough, fear of failure. This short list just scratches the surface, and I have more bad news for you: it is likely that at some point in your life all of your fears will come true. At some time or other, you will probably make a bad decision, make a mistake, look like a fool, feel stupid, and even fail. So how can you prevent that from happening?

You can't. That's life.

Nevertheless, there are some steps you can take that may help prevent your fears from taking over your life and leading to even worse mistakes.

Acknowledge Your Fear

As I said, everyone has fears. There is absolutely nothing wrong with feeling anxiety, especially if it helps you make some decisions and move towards better financial habits. Just acknowledging your fear could help to dissipate it, and move beyond anxiety.

Research Possible Solutions

There is usually more than one right answer. Explore a number of options, make a list, and see which ones might work best for you. There is no better way to face your fears than by acting to find remedies.

Go with Your Gut Instinct

There is a reason so many people talk about "women's intuition." However, we have a tendency to second-guess ourselves, leading to indecision and . . . you guessed it, more fear. Instead, go with your gut. Chances are you may have been right all along.

Prepare and Practice

When you have a big presentation to give, do you sit around worrying over it until the last minute, going into the presentation unprepared? Of course not. You go over your facts and practice your pitch. The same goes for facing down your fears—prepare what you will need in order to take your financial fears by the horns, so to speak, and practice using those tools until you know exactly what you want and how to accomplish it.

Support Yourself

No matter what decision you made or performance you gave, applaud yourself. Reinforce your positive self-image. As I said, we all make mistakes. However, most women are much better at berating themselves when they are wrong than they are at congratulating themselves when they are right. Change that. Be your own biggest fan.

FOUR PORTRAITS

Let's take a moment to revisit the Strong sisters, who are all dealing with their own sets of fears and solutions.

Every month, Wanda finds herself falling further and further behind on her bills. It starts with putting off making her power and water payment on time; and before long, Wanda finds that she is delaying more and more bills simply because she doesn't have the funds to cover them. Soon, she is getting calls from her daughter's college saying that tuition payments are overdue.

Wanda doesn't spend frivolously, but each month it seems that some new expense is popping up—engine trouble on her car, a leaky roof, or some new prescription for her elderly in-laws. Although she tries to sit down and tackle the growing pile of bills, the balance never comes out in her favor.

In order to get through her monthly ritual of sitting at the kitchen table and going through the bills, Wanda has started having a glass of wine to help soften the blows. One glass turns into two, and soon half a bottle is gone. Of course, she doesn't want to drink on an empty stomach, so the wine is accompanied by cheese—which then turns into a chocolate bar. Before long, Wanda can't even face the prospect of her bills without a few drinks and homemade cake.

When she starts to find that some of her clothes are no longer fitting and that her meager wine collection has been decimated, Wanda realizes it's time to take action. She starts to walk in the morning, spending the thirty minutes of "alone time" brainstorming possible ways of bringing in some more money.

Although she doesn't have any firm plans in place, she decides to talk to her children and in-laws, realizing that they need to be aware of the situation. She had wanted to tell them the truth months ago but second-guessed herself, worrying that they wouldn't understand or wouldn't want to help. Much to her surprise and relief, her son and daughter are eager to pitch in wherever they can while the in-laws are certainly sympathetic. Wanda is pleased and realizes she doesn't have to drink alone just to get through her dreaded monthly accounting. It's a slow start, but it's something.

Debbie, on the other hand, refuses to acknowledge that she is in financial trouble. Having received a substantial settlement during her divorce, she tells herself she has plenty saved in the bank. Nonetheless, every month she finds herself dipping into her savings account more and more in order to cover her basic necessities and medical bills.

When the bills start piling up, Debbie simply sells off some bonds. The money is enough to get her through another few months, but before long she is back at her savings account. The truth of her situation hits her when she checks her accounts online and sees that the balance is much less than she was expecting. Could she have really gone through so much money in such a short period of time? Debbie thinks back on her recent expenses and can't think of any extravagant purchases, but she has been forced to see her doctor more frequently lately.

Although not quite ready to face balancing her checkbook, Debbie does acknowledge that she is getting deeper into a bad situation. With her savings depleted, she absolutely must find some alternative incomes. Sitting down at her desk, Debbie makes a list of some possible methods for drumming up extra dollars. Although she likes the idea of starting an online business, she balks. She really knows nothing about computers or online commerce and worries that she could be getting in over her head. However, out of all of her options, it is the one that feels the most right to her.

Debbie isn't quite ready to jump into the world of Internet business just yet, but she does decide to learn more about it, just in case. The decision is enough to encourage her to finally take a frank look at her finances. After all, if she is serious about changing the direction of her business, she will need to know exactly what is in her accounts—no more sticking her head in the sand.

At the same time, Marilyn becomes discouraged when she takes in the whole picture of her financial situation. Everything is in her husband's name, and she knows absolutely nothing about finance. How in the world is she ever going to learn enough to put together her own savings? Is it even necessary? Marilyn begins to think that her whole idea for creating her own nest egg was silly and reactive. After all, her marriage is happy, her husband is healthy, and every indication points to them living a long and well-funded retirement together.

Starting to doubt her own plan, Marilyn grows frustrated and antsy. She needs to get out of the house and decides that a lunch and shopping outing with some of her girlfriends is just the thing to cheer her up. At one of the high-end stores she frequents, Marilyn buys several new dresses she knows look great on her. They are all quite expensive, but Marilyn knows her husband has several business functions coming up, and she rationalizes the purchases by claiming she needs to look her best for all of them.

Marilyn is back in the stores a few days later, this time buying some new appliances for her kitchen. The ones she and her husband have are so outdated, and, she tells herself, she has been meaning to refresh them for a while.

Over the next several weeks, Marilyn continues to shop. She and her husband are more than comfortable, so the cost isn't a problem, but pretty soon even Marilyn's kids are commenting on how many purchases she has made lately. Like the kitchen appliances, Marilyn is able to rationalize all of them, but she doesn't admit to herself the real reason behind her new—and expensive—activity.

The truth is, when Marilyn is shopping she doesn't have to think about her defunct plans to create her own savings. Shopping, unlike finance, is something Marilyn has always enjoyed and been good at, so why not spend her free time buying things for herself and the people she loves—it's not as though she can't afford it.

The truth hits Marilyn when she receives a bill for one of her department store credit cards. She can barely believe her eyes. Has she really spent that much money at a single store? Even worse, the bill is for only one retailer. How much has she spent at other places?

The shock forces Marilyn to realize that her shopping has grown out of control. The next morning, she cancels her plans to go to the mall with some of her girlfriends and instead sits down to take an honest look at exactly what she doesn't know about finance. Making a list of subjects she doesn't understand or hasn't taken the time to learn, she finally takes her first steps towards making her financial future more secure.

Finally, baby sister Sara seems to have her finances in order, but when she really stops to think about her future retirement—despite it being years away—she feels a niggling sense of unease in the back of her mind. She knows she should take the time to go over her savings and pension plan, but she keeps putting off the task.

Finding herself increasingly restless, she picks up an old habit she hasn't given into since her college days— smoking. It's easy enough to get back into the addiction, taking her smoking breaks with the other members of her company unable to break themselves of the habit. She knows she could be spending those breaks getting her retirement plans in order, but occupying those short minutes chatting with her colleagues and indulging in her craving helps to calm the anxieties sitting in the pit of her stomach.

It's the same story when she gets home at night. After eating dinner, the temptation of a cigarette overcomes any thoughts of sitting down at her computer and getting her financials in order. The smoking helps to calm her nerves and gives her hands something to do when she knows they should be flying across a keyboard tracking down all of her retirement funds. As she smokes, Sara discovers it's easy to explain away her fears—she's too young to be worrying about retirement; she has a good job and the retirement money will take care of itself in her pension plan; once she gets that promotion she's been waiting months for, she can finally start putting a little more aside.

However, when Sara realizes that she is now up to a pack a day, she knows something has to change. Investing in some nicotine patches, she discovers that without the smoking breaks, she has no excuse for not taking the time to sit down and go over her retirement plan—even more so after the promotion she had been hoping to get goes to another (male) colleague. As in the case of her sisters, it's a small step, but Sara has finally come to understand that if she doesn't secure her retirement, no one else will either.

For the Strong sisters, the first step is figuring out what exactly retirement means to them. That goes for you, too. In this book, I'm going to share seven simple steps of retirement survival with you—the same steps I've shared with all my clients over the years. These clients are women who, just like the Strongs, overcome their fear and anxiety to create years that are truly golden. I want to show you how not to simply *survive* your retirement . . . but to thrive in it.

Let's start with Step One: crafting a vision.

REFERENCES:

1 Norris, Cathy A. "Retirement Concerns Generally Weigh Heavy for Women." February 2009. http://www.babm.com/strategicplanning/Retirement-Concerns-Generally-Weigh-Heavy-for-Women.htm.

2 Ibid.

3 "Average Cost of U.S. Health Coverage per Employee Is Expected to Cross the $10,000 Threshold for the First Time in 2012, According to Aon Hewitt." PR Newswire. October 2011. http://www.prnewswire.com/news-releases/average-cost-of-us-health-coverage-per-employee-is-expected-to-cross-the-10000-threshold-for-the-first-time-in-2012-according-to-aon-hewitt-130847468.html.

4 "The Real Cost of Higher Education." http://www.savingforcollege.com/tutorial101/the_real_cost_of_higher_education.php.

Chapter 3

Step One:
Crafting a Vision

The first step in a good retirement plan is much like the beginning of any journey—figuring out where you are and where you want to go. Every woman has different needs and goals, and each is in a unique situation.

The Strong sisters are no exception. Wanda wants to finish putting her kids through school and still have enough left over to live comfortably in her later years. Debbie wants to continue earning money and make sure she has enough to cover her future medical costs. Marilyn wants to put some money aside as an emergency nest egg in case anything should happen to her husband. Sara wants to make sure she has enough money to retire on schedule and spend more time with her increasingly enjoyable hobby: knitting.

Everyone has a different picture of what retirement looks like, but in order to make yours happen, you have to know what your unique vision of the future is. When I initially meet with a client, my first question is always: "Where do you want to be in one, three, five, and ten years down the line? What is your vision for your life?"

Often, women underestimate themselves with limiting beliefs. They don't think there is any way that they can earn $500,000 in the next ten years. But if they think like that, it becomes a self-fulfilling prophecy. Not that you need to start a multibillion-dollar corporation, but whatever your vision of your life might be—whether it's putting your kids through college or being able to keep up your weekly Night Out with the girls, you shouldn't think it's an impossible goal. Just remember to always aim high, because if you fall short of your target, at least you'll be better off than when you started.

Of course, all of this talk about aiming high isn't much good without some practicalities to back it up. That's why an important first step in creating your vision is to do some calculations.

ACCUMULATION AND DISTRIBUTION

There are actually two phases to crafting your vision and retirement planning in general. The first is called *accumulation.* This is the time of your life when you are still working: you are saving in your retirement plan and accumulating wealth. It is critical that you accumulate (save) as much wealth as you possibly can during your working years, because you will need it more than you realize later on.

The second phase is called *distribution.* This is the time during your retirement when you distribute your savings to yourself to live on. You withdraw from your retirement plan and savings to supplement your other income(s) and sustain your lifestyle.

In the 1990s, financial advisor William Bengen studied the question of how much a retiree can withdraw from his or her portfolio annually without having that money run out on them. His answer to the problem has become known as the "4% Rule," which states that if you withdraw 4 percent of your initial retirement portfolio plus inflation, annually, your portfolio will probably last thirty years.[1]

It's a good rule of thumb, but one that should be followed with some caution. Outliving your money creates a severe financial crisis that usually occurs in your oldest years—when you are too aged to work. To avoid this, and increase your probability of financial success in your golden years, plan on withdrawing just 2 to 3 percent of your savings in the early years of your retirement.

I have seen many people—both men and women—who, because of job loss, retired prematurely on what they thought was enough money to last them a lifetime only to learn too late that they had overestimated the strength of their portfolio. One of the most important aspects of crafting your vision is being realistic about what you have (accumulation) and what you are intending to spend in your retirement years (distribution).

Accumulation

Retirement can be very much like a camping adventure during an unexpected snowstorm. It can last much longer than you expect, and you must ensure that you have enough supplies.

So let's take inventory of your retirement "supplies," also known as "assets."

INVENTORY OF RETIREMENT ASSETS

Dated_____

Cash and CDs   _____
Savings   _____
Retirement Plan, 401(k) Plan   _____
All IRAs   _____
Pension, if Expected   _____
Stocks   _____
Bonds   _____
Annuities   _____
Social Security   _____
Insurance Settlement or Payouts   _____
Inheritance   _____
Other Expected Income   _____
Home Equity   _____
Other Real Estate Equity   _____
TOTAL ASSETS   _____

*Next, add up your total debt
(also known as liabilities) and
subtract it from your total assets.*

Mortgage # 1   _____
Mortgage # 2   _____
Home Equity Line of Credit   _____
All Credit Cards   _____
College Loans   _____
Other Indebtedness   _____
TOTAL DEBT   _____

Total Assets   _____
Minus Total Debt (Liabilities)   _____
Equals Total Net Retirement Assets
(or **TOTAL NET WORTH**)   _____

These assets are the retirement "supplies" that must last for twenty to forty years. Retirement will last longer than you expect, and your "supplies" may get depleted. If you start now, you can stock up on the savings and investments that you will need to carry you through retirement.

Most people don't know how much they have. That's just a plain fact. You might be surprised at how many people leave IRAs behind in a bank or with a previous employer and never check on them. However, you need to think of your accounts like children—if you don't keep an eye on them they go astray. Don't let your IRAs become forgotten children. You must sit down and look at your accounts at least quarterly in order to know what you have and what you owe. It is a matter of your well-being.

An important first step can be consulting a financial advisor. Working with a competent, experienced financial advisor has many benefits. Her knowledge and expertise can help you understand investments and avoid mistakes. According to a 2011 Wells Fargo Advisors Study, 46 percent of pre-retiree women have financial advisors, and 61 percent of retired women rely on financial advisors for their planning needs.[2] And, according to the same study, half (52 percent) of pre-retirees with an advisor say they are well-prepared financially for retirement, compared to 38 percent of those without.

A financial advisor can help you create a financial plan, a critical tool to get you started on the right path.

According to a 2010 Wells Fargo Retirement Study, "Those who are very confident that they will have saved enough to live the lifestyle they want in retirement are more than twice as likely as those who are not confident to have detailed written plans for retirement."[3] The 2010 Retirement Confidence Survey of the Employee Benefit Research Institute (EBRI) states that "forty-six percent of workers have taken the time and effort to complete a retirement needs calculation—the basic planning step that can help individuals determine how much money they are likely to need in retirement and how much they will need to save to meet that goal."[4]

Those who have done so tend to be "considerably more confident than those who have not about their ability to reach their goal, despite the fact that those doing a calculation name higher retirement savings goals. Twenty-five percent who have done a calculation, compared with eleven percent who have not, say they are very confident that they will be able to accumulate the amount they need."

Financial advisors have years of experience and work in the financial markets every day, while you work at your specialized job. They are uniquely qualified and experienced in investments and different economic cycles to help you make wise investment choices. Financial advisors are more accessible and affordable than you may realize. They can help you identify your retirement goals and tolerance for market risk, and then start you on a plan to reach your retirement goals. Ask your friends and family for referrals for financial advisors. Then interview the various financial advisors to see who is knowledgeable and who will be a good fit for you.

Looking back at the Strong sisters, all four know what they want but now have to do some research to see what needs to be accomplished in order to make their visions a reality. Wanda decides to go through all of her husband's old files to see what accounts they may have forgotten about over the hectic years of work and child-rearing. Debbie, on the other hand, calculates the value of everything she received during her divorce and, for the first time, figures out exactly how much she has left from the original settlement.

Marilyn begins the lengthy process of separating her assets from her husband's—at least on paper—and taking stock of the resources and finances she could reliably count on were something to happen to her spouse. Finally, Sara calculates the totals for all of her accounts—including her current pension plan as well as an IRA she rolled over from a previous employer. For each of the sisters, it is an eye-opening experience that gives them a very real sense of what they will need in order to live comfortably for the next several decades.

Of course, taking inventory is only the first half of the equation. The second may involve a little more legwork.

Distribution

If you want to retire at sixty-five, you are likely now in your peak earning years—how much do you have saved? And how much will you be able to live on in retirement? Personally, I don't want to scrimp in retirement. There are many ways to get to the number you will need, but it's a number that's going to vary from person to person, place to place.

The question to ask yourself is this: How much do I need to retire? Given the lifestyle you want to lead in retirement, will you need $350,000? $500,000? $1,000,000? $3,000,000? Does accumulating that much money make you want to rush right back into denial? I'm not saying everyone can, but let's entertain the possibility.

As I mentioned above, most women don't think it's doable, but I want you to consider it. If you stop now and think about how much you need in order to live abundantly in retirement, even if you are sixty, you can do something about getting to that number every day. Keeping this in mind during the next step is the most necessary—and possibly the hardest.

Here is where working with a financial advisor can really help. Most likely, she will have the expertise and resources, such as computerized software programs that project cash flows and income into the future, to help you determine how much you might need for retirement.

The most common approach to determining how

much you will need for distribution in your later years is to use a percentage (usually 60 to 85 percent) of your income. The theory is that you won't need one hundred percent of your salary because you won't have all the work expenses, such as commuting costs, clothing and cleaners, eating out, paying payroll taxes, or contributing to your 401(k). Keep in mind that you still need to factor in inflation and health care, but more on that later. Make an educated guess about how long you expect to live in retirement, based on your current health or your family history. If you don't know, use thirty years as a placeholder to err on the side of conservatism.

Let's say you earn $75,000 per year after taxes and that you will need 80 percent of your income to live on in retirement. That means you will need $60,000 per year after taxes.

$$\$75,000 \times 0.80 = \$60,000$$

So you will need after-tax income of $60,000 per year for thirty years after you stop working, a.k.a., retire. *Ideally*, we would prefer to invest our savings into something relatively safe, like bonds, and live off of the interest forever. In that way, we would preserve the principal. To put that in perspective, if you had $1,500,000 in municipal bonds that earned 4 percent tax-free interest, you would generate $60,000 per year.

$1,500,000 x .04 = $60,000

In this scenario, you would have enough saved to generate $60,000 after taxes and not have to spend any of the principal, assuming you could get 4 percent from your municipal bonds.

Of course, as I mentioned above, these numbers are going to be different for everyone. Wanda, for example, only makes $50,000 annually and wants to have a little extra in her retirement fund to do some traveling once the kids are done with college. Debbie's income can vary drastically from year to year, depending on her client list, and she needs to make sure she'll have enough to cover some of her more costly prescriptions.

Marilyn doesn't have any of her own income at all and knows she has to take her children's school tuition into account. Sara earns a healthy six-figure salary but also has high work-related expenses, though she dreams of a second home some place with palm trees and sandy beaches.

Each Strong sister will certainly have a different amount accumulated and their individual visions for the future will be equally varying, but having made an accounting of their current assets, all four women must now try to figure out how much they will yet need to prevent those dreams from fading away in the light of financial reality.

A different but equally essential method to securing financial success in retirement is to create several income streams, and "stack" them, until you reach $60,000 in annual income, but I'll explore that more in later chapters. For now, the most important thing to remember is that you need some idea of the resources you have and how those resources can help you accumulate the funds you will need over the twenty-five to thirty years of retirement. Keep in mind, however, that these are far from fixed numbers.

FUZZY NUMBERS AND INFLATION

Unfortunately, the example above does not take inflation into account. People may understand what inflation is, but most underestimate the effect it will have on their retirement savings.

The Consumer Price Index (CPI) is a measure of inflation. It keeps track of the prices on food, clothing, gasoline, and other consumer goods. The twenty-five year CPI has averaged 2.5 percent per year, and the fifty-year CPI has averaged 4 percent per year.[5] That means that the cost of things we use every day has gone up by 2.5 percent every year for the past twenty-five years, and by 4 percent on average over the past fifty years.

A 3 percent inflation rate over thirty years will reduce your purchasing power by half, so that at the beginning of your retirement you may be able to live on $60,000 per year, but by the end of your thirty-year retirement, you will need $120,000 per year just to maintain the same standard of living.[6] This particularly affects women because of our longevity and the fact that we generally receive little or no life-sustaining pension.

Let's put this in perspective. Compare the prices of the following over the last thirty to forty years:

- A postage stamp when you were a child to the current postal rate.
- A hamburger, shake, and fries when you were ten to the price today.
- A gallon of gas when your parents were driving you to school to the price today.
- A gallon of milk when you were in kindergarten to the price today.
- A pair of blue jeans when you started school to today.

Now let's look at how much your income will grow over the thirty to forty years of your retirement. Compare the following based on your knowledge or expectations:

- The annual income from your pension when you start your retirement to the expected annual income thirty years later.
- The value of your Social Security income when you start your retirement to the expected income you will receive at age eighty-five.

Inflation also affects your investments. Here's how. Let's say you earn 8 percent return on your investments, and inflation is at 3 percent. Your real rate of return, after inflation is figured in, is only 5 percent. That is because we subtract inflation from your return.

8% investment return - 3% inflation =
5% real rate of return

If you have enough saved that you can withdraw less than THREE percent in retirement, your principal is expected to be safe and intact. However, if you must withdraw 5 percent or more in order to live a sustainable lifestyle, you are likely to need to spend down your principal over the course of your retirement lifetime. If you spend it down too fast, chances are strong that you may run out of money.

So how do you know if you are spending down too fast? This is a very good question. In fact, it is a *critical question*. Take your life savings, however you define it. If you don't know, use the sum total of your retirement plan accounts, such as your 401(k) and IRAs. Next, write down how much you are spending each year. Now divide your annual spending by your life savings.

Annual Spending _____
÷ Life Savings _____
= Spend-down rate _____

That is your spend-down rate. Is it more than 4 percent? If it is, then it's time to start figuring out ways to increase your savings now and your income after retirement. It's all part of crafting the vision.

I know that this all seems very technical right now, especially if you haven't had any experience with financial planning, but that's why it's important to start considering these things *immediately*—whether you have twenty years or two months until retirement. It's never too early. Likewise, it's never too late. In fact, as I'll explore in the next chapter, time can be more of a friend than an enemy.

REFERENCES:

1 Krueger, Cheryl. "'4% Rule' Serves as Guideline for Today's Retirees, But Use With Caution." April 4, 2012. http://www.huffingtonpost.com/cheryl-krueger/retirement-planning-four-percent-rule_b_1404026.html.

2 "Collective Wisdom: Women's Retirement Trends and Insights," 2011 Wells Fargo Advisors Study. http://blog.wellsfargo.com/retirement/docs/womensbrochure.pdf.

3 2010 Wells Fargo Retirement Study. http://blog.wellsfargo.com/retirement/docs/2010%20WF_retirement%20study_fin.pdf.

4 "The 2010 Retirement Confidence Survey: Confidence Stabilizing, But Preparations Continue to Erode." EBRI Issue Brief #340, Employee Benefit Research Institute: March 2010.

5 Bureau of Labor Statistics, United States Department of Labor. www.bls.gov/cpi/.

6 Dennis, Keith. "Inflation and the Erosion of Your Income." March 14, 2012. http://annuities.about.com/b/2012/03/14/inflation-and-the-erosion-of-your-income.htm.

Chapter 4

Step Two:
Making Time Your Friend

In today's world, women are often bombarded with images about the ravages of time: anti-aging creams, biological clocks, and the pressures to have it all—a career and family—by the ripe old age of thirty-five. Time can often seem like the enemy, but you can make time your friend—in many cases, you have much more time than it might at first appear. If you are in your twenties or thirties, you have three decades to put plans for retirement into place, and if you have already reached the retirement threshold, you have the free time needed to make a new plan work.

Currently, 42 percent of women claim they don't know how to reach their retirement needs.[1] They think they don't have enough time to set a plan in motion, either because they are too busy dealing with the issues of daily life or because they believe they have passed the point of no return, so to speak.

However, harnessing the power of time is easy enough if you take the proper steps: *Decide, Learn, Research, Plan, Act, Use the power of now, Use the power of time for compounding,* and *Keep a log.* Let's take a look at each one of these and see how, when combined, they can help you make the ticking clock your ally.

Decide

It may seem like an obvious statement, but the first step is deciding to change your retirement outlook and improve your security. After all, nothing changes until you make a decision. Don't be deceived, though. Making a firm decision can be much harder than it initially appears.

For example, when a smoker says, "I want to quit smoking," that's one thing, but until he or she actually *decides* to do it, that statement doesn't mean much. Once the decision is made, that person's entire world changes, but the first step is getting in the mindset.

Likewise, the very fact that you are reading this book is proof that you have come to some sort of decision about your retirement and are now ready to follow through on it, which brings us to the next step . . .

Learn

Once the decision has been made to take active steps in improving your retirement outlook, the next stage is to learn all you can about retirement plans, investments, and projected income needs. If you've already done the "Crafting a Vision" phase, then you are definitely on the right path. You have an idea of where you are heading and what you will need to get there, but the next big question is *how*.

The answer is financial literacy—learning about your money and the unique financial situation you are in.

In the end, that's what we're talking about and what most women lack. In fact, in a study done by Mahnaz Mahdavi, director of the Center for Women and Financial Independence at Smith College, the mean financial literacy test score for women with at least a bachelor's degree is only 47 percent.[2] That's a worryingly low number, but one of the ways you can keep from becoming part of that statistic is to educate yourself.

Financial literacy is a fairly complex concept, which may be part of the intimidation factor for most women. However, if you stop and think about it, women have gained literacy in a variety of incredibly complex areas over the last few decades. How many women have learned how to use smartphones just to keep in touch with their children or grandchildren? What about computers? Or calculating caloric intakes?

These are all areas that might be considered outside the normal realm for a woman, but they take the time to learn about them because circumstances force them into it. In the same way, finance may initially seem like something daunting and beyond your scope. You don't think you can learn about it, let alone conquer it. According to a report prepared by Prudential, over 80 percent of women feel they need some kind of help in making wise financial decisions.[3]

Nevertheless, when all is said and done, literacy is nothing more than reading up on a subject. Start small—you don't need to go out and buy every book on financial planning published in the last ten years, but maybe read the *Wall Street Journal* every day and look up any of the terminology you don't understand.

Financial literacy is just like any new subject; start slow and before you know it, you'll be gaining knowledge and preparing yourself for the next phase of making time your friend.

Research

Once you have done some reading and are more familiar with the parlance of financial literacy, the next step is to research some methods of creating income for your retirement. Start by doing some market research.

Let's say you are considering turning your knitting

skills towards opening a store exclusively for the purpose of selling green socks. But is there a market for it in your area? Would it be better to start online before renting a store space? Is there some place in the continental United States that might have much more of a demand for green socks? Or perhaps you are working on a plan that involves selling products to China? How much would it cost to get your products there? Is it even feasible, and can you make a profit? Do some market research; figure out exactly what would be involved with making your idea a reality.

In today's society, the first place many people would look for information is the Internet; there is simply a wealth of data and research there. Between Google, YouTube, Yahoo!, and Ask.com, you can type in just about any question and receive an answer. We use it all the time for things like information on how to change a tire. Why not for market research as well?

Having said that, I always like to advise my clients not to discount more traditional sources. Personally, I love reference librarians. You could ask them any question and they would be able to tell you where to find the information. Beyond the library and the Internet, there are a variety of other ways to find the data you might need, so be sure not to overlook something just because it may be outside your usual methods. No matter what, however, make sure you have all the pertinent information before undertaking anything.

Let's take a moment to look at an example from the investment world, specifically bonds: I once had a client in her eighties who had very little income, so she was in a low-income tax bracket, but who had managed to save quite a bit over the course of her life. She didn't have a pension, and as a result she was forced to become more frugal as she got older.

In order to try and supplement her savings, she decided that she wanted municipal bonds because you don't have to pay taxes on them. I explained to her that, because she was in a low tax bracket, she would make more money from the corporate bonds even after paying taxes on the interest. In the end, she got her corporate bonds and it all worked out well enough for her, but that is the kind of thing you would want to research before jumping into it—finding out what type of bonds, if any, would be a viable solution for you and your situation.

As illustrated in the example of my low-tax-bracket client, municipal bonds are more appropriate for investors in a high tax bracket, because what you keep after taxes depends on your tax bracket. Municipal bonds do not make sense for investors in low tax brackets, who are usually better off with corporate bonds. Had my client done more research, she would have realized that.

Here is how to determine which bond, the taxable corporate bond or the tax-free municipal bond, is better for you, given your tax bracket, assuming that the bonds are of equivalent quality.

First, you find the after-tax yield of the taxable corporate bond, or what interest you would receive after taxes are taken into account. Then you compare the after-tax yield of the corporate bond to the tax-free yield of the tax-exempt municipal bond. All other factors being equal, such as quality and duration of the bonds, the bond that gives you the most interest after taxes is the type of bond that you should consider investing in.

Here's an example. Say you're in the 35 percent tax bracket and you are presented with the choice of buying either a AAA-rate corporate bond paying 7 percent taxable interest, or a AAA-rated municipal bond paying 5 percent tax-exempt interest. Which bond should you buy?

Taxable equivalent yield of municipal bond = the tax-exempt (municipal) yield divided by (100% minus your tax bracket).

After-tax yield of corporate bond = corporate bond yield x (100% minus your tax bracket).

Taxable corporate bond:
6.00% x (100% - 35%) = 6.00 x (.65) = 3.90%

Tax-free municipal bond:
4.00% tax-free

This means that after you pay taxes, you only get to keep 3.90 percent interest income on the corporate bond. The triple tax-free municipal bond paying 4.00 percent tax-exempt interest is a better investment if you're in the 35 percent tax bracket.

What if you're in the 10 percent tax bracket?

Taxable corporate bond:
6.00% x (100% - 10%) = 6.00 x .90 = 5.40% after taxes

Tax-free municipal bond:
4.00% tax-free

In that case, you get to keep 5.40 percent interest income on the corporate bond after taxes are factored in versus 4.00 percent on the municipal bond. Clearly, the corporate bond would be a better investment if you're in the 10 percent tax bracket.

The tax equivalent yield tells you what yield you would need to receive on a taxable corporate bond to match the tax-free yield of the municipal bond. The tax equivalent yield is calculated by dividing the tax-free municipal yield by (100% minus your tax bracket). For example, let's say you could get 5% on a tax-free municipal bond and you're in the 35% tax bracket. What is the yield you would need to receive on the corporate bond (the tax equivalent yield) to match the tax-free yield of the municipal bond?

Tax equivalent yield = Tax-free municipal bond yield
                            (100% minus your tax bracket)

$$7.69\% = \frac{5\%}{(100\%-35\%)} = \frac{5}{.65}$$

This is the kind of research you would need to do before jumping into the world of bonds—the kind of research that should accompany any financial decision.

Plan

Make one. Write it down. Stick to it. If you don't know how to create a financial plan, consult a financial advisor. Again, they are more accessible than you think.

As I mentioned in earlier chapters, one of the most important things you can do when beginning to plan for your financial future is to sit down and ask yourself where you are heading. Where do you want to be five or ten years down the line? Next, strategize—figure out *how* that is going to happen. How will you get there?

Some women decide that they will downsize their house, use their savings to buy dividend stocks, or rent out their extra bedrooms in order to get another line of cash flow going. If you're not sure what your plan is, look at the result you want and then reverse engineer. Again, avoid thinking that you can't achieve your goal. Just be willing to open your mind to any possibility, and then, visualize a fantastic "what if?" We don't know where life is going to take us, but opportunities open up when you try.

Once you have a plan in mind, write it down and put it everywhere: in the kitchen, in your purse, on your vanity mirror—anywhere you might spot it throughout the day. That way, you will keep it fresh and motivating. "Out of sight, out of mind" may be a cliché, but it's also a truism. If you have that card in your purse, then you can pull it out when you get low. Or if it's taped to your bathroom mirror, you can look at it each morning so that it will be in your mind throughout the day.

Act

Do something every day to improve your retirement prospects. It could be something as simple as reading the *Wall Street Journal* and trying to increase your financial literacy, or it could be researching a product you want to invest in, or even a product you want to create. If you've decided to rent out space, maybe your one daily act is calling the painters to get the upstairs bedrooms spruced up.

Whatever it might be, take one step each day in moving your plan forward. Day by day by day. In that way, you'll keep the excitement alive. "Yes," you'll be able to tell yourself, "it's possible for me to actually create income for life. Even if it's a small idea, I can stack several of those small ideas until I have enough to sustain me throughout retirement. I have the power to create income in my life through strategies that are viable."

If you take one step each day, you'll keep that momentum moving forward, and before you know it, that plan won't seem quite so impossible anymore.

Use the Power of Now

Do not waste mind-time in frivolous activities, such as chatter or complaining. Your time is a valuable resource, and your mind is your best tool.

During my time in the jewelry industry, I worked a retail job while trying to build my own small business. As a result, while working at my "day job," I would also be thinking about whom I wanted to call on my lunch hour—contacts such as Tiffany and Cartier. Rather than complaining about my current job, which I wasn't fond of, or wasting money going out to eat somewhere, I was using my energy to map out ways to better my current situation.

If you close your eyes and listen, you often hear a lot of complaining, which is nothing more than negative energy. Instead of giving in to it, redirect your "Now" thoughts into things such as "What do I want? Why do I want it? How am I going to get there?"

Of course, it's an evolving process, and the plan you come up with today is not going to be the plan or strategy you will be refining a year from now. That's as it should be, because nothing stays the same. Nothing is static; you must always be tweaking and improving your plan. In fact, you're going to get new ideas as you go along, which will be key in keeping you fresh when you're in the moment. That kind of constant strategizing and revising is much more exciting than the chatter and negativity, not to mention more productive. Rather than focusing on all the naysaying thoughts, you are moving your personal retirement plan forward.

Use the Power of Time for Compounding

Anything you save and invest today can be growing faster due to the wonderful power of compound earnings. Learn about it and harness it.

Many times, women are too worried to take a good look at their mortgage or, in the case of younger women, their student loans. For them, "compounding" may be a dirty word, something to be feared. But that doesn't have to be the case.

In truth, anything you save and invest today can be growing faster due to the wonderful power of compound earnings. This is the secret of how "money goes to money," and how the rich get richer. "Compound earnings" is a technical term that means that when you save and invest, your money earns money. When you reinvest the money that you earned, now your earnings are earning money, too. Over time, this is a very effective way of helping your money to grow—as evidenced by the table below.

THE POWER OF COMPOUNDING

This table illustrates the power of compounding with a $10,000 initial investment and an annual return of 6 percent.

YEAR	VALUE
1	10,600
2	11,236
3	11,910
4	12,624
5	13,382
6	14,185
7	15,036
8	15,938
9	16,894
10	17,908
11	18,983
12	20,122
13	21,329
14	22,609
15	23,965
16	25,403
17	26,927
18	28,543
19	30,256
20	32,071

Shapiro, David. *Retirement Countdown: Take Action Now to Get the Life You Want.* Financial Times / Prentice Hall, an imprint of Pearson Education; copyright 2004, Upper Saddle River, New Jersey, 07458; pp.350-353.

By allowing the earnings to be reinvested and *also* earn the assumed rate of 6 percent, over twenty years, the initial investment of $10,000 more than tripled to $32,071, not including taxes!

That's the power of compounding and tax deferral. Compounding is something you can make work *for* you simply by understanding it, by lassoing it in and taking the first step. I will agree that it's not an easy road, and in the early years of saving, you won't see the compounding as clearly. In later years, though, it can be extremely effective.

Keep a Log

Journal your process and success. Doing so will help you see what you are accomplishing on a daily basis—what works and what doesn't.

The most important thing to remember at this point is that you will make mistakes. I recently spoke with a woman who was trying to build up her own small jewelry design business. Hoping to sell some of her work at a local art fair, she had rented booth space. However, the entire venture had cost her more than she had expected, and her sales for the day were far below what she had hoped. She was traumatized by the whole experience, but I advised her not to give up. The art fair had been a learning experience, one that would help her craft a stronger business plan in the future.

Nevertheless, in order to really make the most of the incident, the jewelry artist should write it down in a log, the better to build her position in the long term. The process of writing it down will help her to analyze it and distance herself from it emotionally, so that it becomes more of an examination rather than a deflating experience.

Rather than saying, "I spent all this money on a booth at the art fair and it didn't pay off," she can scrutinize the situation and say, "Was it the right art fair? Right size booth? Right time of year?" Those things come to light when you write it down and start to analyze it, as opposed to just beating yourself up about all the money that was lost.

On the flip side, keeping a log can be a source of encouragement as well. You can write down all of your successes, such as "Today I got an order for one thousand little widgets," or "Today I showcased some of my goods," or "Today I got a roommate." Whatever your victory might be, it's those successes that will carry you forward, and writing them down works as a reminder that you are on the right track.

PLANS IN ACTION

Let's take another look at the Strong sisters in order to see how these steps might work in various scenarios. Wanda, having calculated how much she will need to see her kids through college with enough left over to live comfortably through her retirement years, realizes her savings isn't going to get the job done on its own. She is going to need another source of income, though she certainly doesn't want to be working into her eighties.

Instead, she checks out a few books on financial planning from her local library and starts up a dialogue with her daughter, who is majoring in business and can clarify some of the concepts Wanda doesn't immediately understand.

Having informed herself a bit more in the area of financial literacy, Wanda decides that one way of generating more income would be to rent out the two bedrooms once used by her children before they left for college. Before she plunges into the role of landlord, however, she does a little research to see what kind of a market there might be for rental space in her neighborhood. It's a quiet suburban street, and she's not sure how many people would be interested in renting rooms so far away from the downtown area—where most of the single career-minded tend to gravitate.

Nevertheless, she discovers that a number of students at a nearby art college are always looking for reasonable living space, so Wanda starts making up some flyers. Each day she sets a new task for herself—whether it be going to the printer to print off the flyers or using her lunch hour to hang a few of them up at the art school.

She is constantly thinking and strategizing, keeping track of all of her thoughts in a special business journal she started just for this venture.

Within a month she has several applications for possible tenants, though it takes her another week of meeting with the students and finding which ones would be the best fit for her house—including her work schedule and the needs of her husband's elderly parents—until she settles on two renters.

Wanda is far from done with her planning—in fact, she is starting to research the world of stocks and bonds—but she is satisfied at having taken the first steps in working out her retirement goals.

Likewise, Debbie knows she has to start figuring out ways to fund her health care coverage in the years when she is likely to need it the most. Debbie has never considered herself good with finance-speak, so her first step is to start reading the *Wall Street Journal* every day in order to familiarize herself with the language.

Once she feels she has a better grasp on the world of finance, she begins researching some options for business loans. Despite having spent years operating her small company, she has never really put together a practical business plan. Now, however, she knows she can delay no longer.

Determined to organize her business—just as she has been saying she would for years—Debbie makes a list of things that have to get done in order for her new business plan to really take hold: contacts to be called, advertising to arrange, and a website to set up. Knowing she is the kind of person who can get excited about a plan one day and completely forget about it by morning, Debbie makes copies of her list and sticks them to her bathroom mirror, bedside lamp, and refrigerator door.

In addition to the loan, she starts looking into options for turning her somewhat meager savings to her advantage, of compounding the interest in order to build on what she already has in the bank. It will be a slow process, she knows, but it will pay off eventually.

Each evening, Debbie sits at her kitchen table and writes down everything she has accomplished that day, both the good and the bad. Initially, it isn't always a pretty picture—especially the state of Debbie's accounts—but eventually things begin to even out as Debbie gets a handle on both her business and her financial literacy. For the first time, she is relieved, seeing a light at the end of the tunnel for her retirement dilemmas.

Marilyn, on the other hand, has no idea where to start. Although she has always handled the household budget and accounts, it is her husband who has kept track of their larger investments, retirement plans, and savings accounts.

Deciding she needs to understand more about their financial situation if she wants to save up her own nest egg, Marilyn enrolls in a finance class at the local community college. Before long, she is studying up on her husband's IRA and 401(k) plans while researching methods that would allow her to set up her own savings accounts. Terminology and figures that might as well have been Greek to her before are now making sense and Marilyn realizes that the best way to grow her personal savings is through investments.

With the help of a financial advisor, Marilyn researches various companies and products until settling on her investment choices. Each day, she makes a point of following their progress on the market and making notes on other investment possibilities in her journal. Before she knows it, Marilyn's husband is coming to *her* for financial advice, and the future is looking much less intimidating.

Finally, Sara already considers herself fairly financially savvy, keeping up with the world of finance at large as well as her own retirement accounts. However, even she admits that there is still quite a bit she doesn't know. Most important, she has recently been considering starting a small Internet arts business for some of her knitting pieces. However, she has no idea how to go about it.

Doing some research and even asking her sister Debbie for advice, Sara begins to form a plan of action. Rather than spending her lunch hours chatting with the other junior executives at the coffee shop down the street, she uses the hour to do some market research online, looking into websites such as Etsy and Amazon in order to learn if there is even a market for her knit products.

When she discovers that online sales of knitted items are currently higher than ever, she writes down her plan of action—which includes a nightly knitting schedule and some more research, this time into online sales practices.

Her business is still a long way from becoming a reality, but Sara feels as though she has a good grasp on the work yet to do. While keeping her "day job," she is ready to embark on a new business venture, and one that could help secure her retirement funds.

In each of these cases, the Strong sisters use their specific talents and situations to make time work in their favor. They made decisions, educated themselves, and took action—whether it was youngest sister Sara putting together a long-term business plan for her knitting or oldest sibling Wanda using her house as a resource for bringing in more income. Suddenly, time is no longer the enemy but a tool to be harnessed in preparation for the next step—developing a solid plan of action based on facts, not fear.

REFERENCES:

1 "What about Women (and Retirement)?" ING Retirement Revealed Study. http://ing.us/rri/publications.

2 Kadlec, Dan. "Women and Money: Even College Grads Flunk Personal Finance." June 28, 2012. http://moneyland.time.com/2012/06/28/women-and-money-even-college-grads-flunk-personal-finance/.

3 "Financial Experience and Behaviors Among Women." 2010-2011 Prudential Research Study. http://www.retirementredzone.prudential.com/media/.../dams_121601.pdf.

Chapter 5

Step Three:
Designing a Fear-Free Plan

When faced with a large debt or the realization that there just isn't enough money in your retirement plan to cover much more than your very basic necessities, it's easy, as discussed in previous chapters, to fall into addictions and escapism that momentarily help you ignore the problems at hand. It can be as seemingly innocent as shopping or more blatantly damaging, such as alcoholism. No matter what, such behavior is fear-induced and harmful.

Maybe you can't face doing your bills without a glass of wine to help prepare yourself for the unpleasant task. Or perhaps you avoid doing your bills until they are late because you are afraid you don't have enough money and you don't know what to do about it. Such reactions are part of soothing the low-level sense of fear that you are falling behind, and, with no ready answers, such behavior can look more appealing than actually dealing with the problem at hand.

As of 2011, nearly 30 percent of women surveyed expressed high levels of anxiety about their finances, compared to only 17 percent of men.[1] There is no denying that women often feel besieged by the financial problems around them, whether it be serious debt or getting their spending under control.

Recently, studies have found that women tend to be overwhelmed by debt more frequently than men; they are more likely to carry a credit card balance over from one month to the next as well as only pay the minimum required by their lender every month.[2] Although this leads to the misconception that women are "bad" with money, that's not always the case. Emergencies arise. Children need school supplies. Elderly parents need medication. The list can go on and on.

The key to overcoming these issues is developing a fear-free plan of action. First and foremost, it's important to acknowledge that you are not alone in these fears. Women across the country and the world suffer from the same insecurities, but a few important steps can help alleviate them.

LEARN THE BASICS OF FINANCE

I have mentioned this numerous times in previous chapters, but it cannot be reiterated enough. Get financially savvy. Go online or to the library and read financial articles, books, and newspapers. Get interested in your own finances—it's not over your head. Dollars and sense—it's new, but not beyond your capability.

A good first step in becoming more finance literate, as was mentioned in Chapter 3, is to get advice from a financial advisor. Why? She is trained in investments and retirement planning and can take an objective look at your money situation, making suggestions that will likely help improve things. She can help you create a financial plan to get you on track for retirement and in the process teach you much of the necessary terminology.

Many women avoid going to see a financial advisor because they don't have any money or are deep in debt and believe they can't afford it, but that's precisely when you should see a financial advisor. Get recommendations from people you respect.

When you call her for an appointment, ask her what she would charge for a consultation and a financial plan. If it is complimentary, as is sometimes the case, go and see her and pick her brain. But be prepared. Bring all your financial statements and be organized so you do not waste her time. Chances are she will give you valuable advice and a direction in which to move. If you feel that your personalities are not a good fit, go and see another financial advisor. You will know instinctively when you are working with the right person.

Organize

Get your office and checkbook in order. Clean out your desk, de-clutter and set up systems. This may seem difficult to those of us who lack that organizational muscle, but it is a muscle we can develop. Take it in very small steps so that you do not become overwhelmed. Clean out just one desk drawer per week. Create one system for incoming bills and another one for your files.

The next phase is to start balancing your checkbook regularly. Few people enjoy spending time on this chore, but it's absolutely necessary in order to maintain a healthy budget. Think of it much like following a diet and exercise plan; keeping regular account of your weight alerts you when there might be a problem and allows you to correct it that much faster. The closer you watch your weight, the easier it is to keep it in a healthy range.

It's the same with your checkbook. The closer you watch your inflows and outflows, the better you stay within your budget. So, balance your checkbook as often as you can—weekly, bi-weekly, or at the very least monthly. Do not go longer than one month—that's a hard and fast rule.

Another task to accomplish as quickly and frequently as possible is opening the mail. This is one thing you can do to really empower yourself. That credit card bill is scary, but it is better to see the devil itself and take action than to live in fear of the unknown. And it will help you to stay on time with your bills. Never, repeat, never be late on your mortgage and credit card bills. Just keep paying the minimum until you can fix your situation. Don't worry, there is a way out.

In fact, one way of staying organized and on top of those bills is by adopting online bill pay, a wonderful method for simplifying your bookkeeping by setting up your bills to go out automatically. There is no reason to ever be late on a bill again. In fact, one of the best features of bill pay is that you can go online at any given moment and check your balance to see which bills have been paid. This is a terrific way of keeping up with your checkbook. Moreover, if you travel, your bills will get paid automatically while you are away. Online bill pay usually costs a few dollars per month, but it will help you manage your checkbook more easily.

Just like every other aspect of this program, these steps will look different for everyone. In the case of Wanda, organizing means cleaning out a corner of her kitchen and setting up a work space, complete with computer, accounting files, and an In/Out box that helps her keep her bills going out on time each month. For Debbie, it's a matter of sitting down with her checkbook and balancing it, down to the penny, for the first time in a year. Marilyn learns how to set up online bill pay and, as a result, streamlines the household budget. Sara makes sure that she stops leaving her pile of mail sitting on the kitchen table and forgetting about it each night after coming home from work.

For each of the sisters, organization entails something different but is equally important to their determination to face their financial futures without fear.

Use Cash Instead of Credit

This may seem like a strange concept to those of us who are used to using plastic, but did you know that when we use cash we spend less?[3] Whenever we whip out the credit cards to make a purchase, it distances us from the actual payment aspect of the exchange—we can enjoy the purchase without having to worry about the consequences, at least until the end of the month.

Using cash, on the other hand, is an immediate reminder of the consequences of our purchase—and sometimes having a reminder can be a good thing. Furthermore, by using cash over credit, you can also alleviate stress in your life by not having to remember how much you put on this credit card or that credit card.

A great first step in getting away from credit is to go back to carrying and using your checkbook—with a running balance—and leaving all those credit cards at home. Although you can hang onto one for emergencies—such as a flat tire—in general you should forget those cards exist.

Next, close out all your retail store credit cards, even if they offer special deals. Those deals are an enticement to spend more than you can afford and are not worth the finance charges. Get off their mailing lists; you don't need the temptation of their sales.

At Wanda's house, all credit cards, with the exception of one, are cut in half. The remaining card is placed in a cup of water in the freezer, only to be broken out, literally, in case of emergencies. Debbie opts to stop using her debit card for anything other than ATM withdrawals, requiring that she carry cash at all times. Marilyn decides to block all of her online shopping sites from the computer while Sara gives up all of her store accounts—she already has plenty of suits for work and that Labor Day sale isn't really *that* much of a bargain. In each case, the Strong sisters are learning how freedom from credit cards can also equal freedom from fear.

Keep Track of Your Spending

Here's a fascinating exercise: write down everything you spend money on for one week. Carry a small notebook in your purse. Then look in your checkbook and credit card statements and write down everything you spent money on for one month. You only have to do this exercise once to have your eyes opened. You will be amazed at how much you are spending and where the money goes!

Next, create a spending plan. Start by writing down how much income you have on a monthly basis. Then decide how you want to spend it. You are in control.

You have choices. The first item you should put on your spending plan is yourself. Always pay yourself first—try to save 10 percent of your income on a regular basis. If that isn't feasible, choose a lesser amount: for example, 1 to 6 percent. However, be sure to pay yourself *something*—it's the start of a good saving habit.

Next, list your mandatory bills, such as rent or mortgage and utilities. Then write down all your other bills. In the case of credit card payments, double up on them—if you can—until you pay them off. Look for ways to cut your expenses. Decide what is important to you. Perhaps you will give up eating out in order to pay down your bills. Or maybe you will do your nails yourself to save a little more money. Try to eliminate as many of the non-essentials as possible.

Wanda throws out all of her takeout menus; Debbie diligently writes down everything she purchases; Marilyn restructures her family's budget; and Sara packs her own lunch—all four women determined to make the most of their cash.

Look for Creative Ways to Increase Your Income

I'll get into this more in the following chapters, but here is the key thing to remember at this point: if you do not have enough money to pay your bills each month, there are only two things you can do. You must either 1) increase your income or 2) reduce your expenses. In all likelihood, it will be some combination of both. No matter how you view it, though, you need to start looking for ways to open up new income streams.

Having gone through all of these steps, it's easy to focus on the negative—what's going wrong with your financial situation. However, it's also important to celebrate your successes, no matter how small. Everything from canceling your department store credit cards to setting up an orderly and timely method for paying your bills should be considered an achievement. Even something as simple as organizing your filing cabinet is a step forward and puts you in a great position to tackle the next step of the process—managing your credit.

REFERENCES:

1 Mac, Ryan. "More Women Report 'Overwhelming Financial Stress,' Survey Finds." June 23, 2011. http://www.bloomberg.com/news/2011-06-23/more-women-report-overwhelming-financial-stress-survey-finds.html.

2 "Credit Card Debt and the Gender Divide." March 8, 2012. http://www.credit.com/blog/2012/05/credit-card-debt-and-the-gender-divide/.

3 "Do We Spend More When We Swipe Plastic?" October 12, 2007. http://poorerthanyou.com/2007/10/12/do-we-spend-more-when-we-use-swipe-plastic/.

Chapter 6

Step Four:
Credit Management Your Mom Would Be Proud Of

In the world of retirement, debt = guilt. You should get rid of both. The two most common forms of debt are credit card and real estate debt, but as a younger generation finishes school only to find diminishing employment opportunities, college and graduate school loans are also becoming an increasing problem.

So how do you ditch the debt?

Some methods seem like simple common sense, such as using your credit cards wisely or, as mentioned in the previous chapter, setting them aside entirely. However, if you really want to help alleviate some of your debt problems, it's important to start thinking outside of the box. In regard to real estate, for example, you might consider a non-traditional living arrangement, such as finding a roommate or, as Wanda Strong has done, renting out a room in your large house.

In fact, not being one to suggest something without having given it a try myself, I admit that I took my own advice and advertised for a roommate. It took me a few months to find someone who I thought would be a good fit, but now we have a happy arrangement that I couldn't be more pleased with. We are both single women with our own lives and careers who happen to share the same condo because it's a financially smart move.

Again, thinking of creative ways to help reduce your debt is a great way of getting yourself back on strong financial footing, but, coming back to that emphasis on financial literacy, it's also important to understand exactly what words like "credit score," "bankruptcy," and "FICO" mean for you.

FICO AND HOW YOUR CREDIT SCORE AFFECTS YOUR FINANCIAL FUTURE

We are constantly bombarded with commercials about the importance of our credit score. Especially recently, it seems that knowing your credit score is more important than remembering your telephone number. However, are you really sure what all of those words the commercials throw around actually mean? Sure, we've all heard FICO more times than anyone would care to remember, but what does it stand for?

FICO is an acronym for Fair Isaac Corporation, which grades you on your credit. Once your score is calculated, FICO sells your information—with your permission, of course—to the credit rating agencies. The credit rating agencies then sell it to the lenders from whom you are applying for credit.

The three major credit rating agencies are Equifax (www.equifax.com), Experian (www.experian.com), and TransUnion (www.transunion.com). These credit rating agencies store the credit reports and scores of millions of Americans just like you. When you apply for a loan, a credit card, or in-store credit, you sign a release that allows the credit agencies to run an updated credit report on you to see if you are secure enough to qualify to purchase your desired item on credit. This might include a home, a car, a flat-screen TV, or a home equity line of credit. It also includes any item purchased on an in-store instant credit card.

Service providers such as insurance companies, public utilities, and phone service providers also use credit scores to see if you are creditworthy enough to rent an apartment, get insurance, and receive utility and phone service. Your credit scores determine what rate you will be charged on your credit cards and loans. Higher credit scores help you to get better credit offers, faster credit approval, and lower interest rates on your credit cards and loans.

So, all in all, pretty important stuff.

FICO scores range from 300 to 850, with 850 being the best. Just as with your GPA when you were in high school, you want high scores. The higher your credit score, the lower the interest rate that you are charged. Obviously, a lower interest rate on your mortgage and credit cards can save you thousands of dollars a year. So it behooves you to keep your FICO score high.

Unfortunately, when you're dealing with debt issues, keeping that credit rating on the rise can be very difficult. Luckily, there are some steps you can take to improve your FICO score.

Pay Your Credit Card Bills in Full Every Month

This will help you avoid incurring finance charges. It's a lesson Wanda Strong learned when she put off making payments to her credit card bill in favor of making sure other bills were sent in on time. Your credit cards may seem like the least important payments when compared with rent and groceries, but the harm an outstanding bill can do to your credit score could last for years.

Establish and Maintain a Good Payment History

Basically, this means that you should always pay your credit card bill on time. Like her sister, Debbie put off paying her credit card bills because there always seemed to be a more pressing expense. As a result, her credit score plummeted and interest rates rose. When deciding to pursue a business loan for her new company, Debbie's first step was paying off those credit card bills and making sure that the few cards she kept were always paid promptly.

If You Cannot Pay Your Credit Card in Full Each Month, Always Pay More Than the Minimum

Did you know that, according to the Consumer Federation of America (www.cfa.org), if you charge a $1,000 item on a credit card with a 19 percent interest rate and pay just the minimum monthly payment of twenty dollars, it will take you over eight years to pay it off—and that is if you never charge another item on that card. Even worse, once all of the interest is calculated in, you will have paid an extra $1,000 for the item.

Sara Strong learned this the hard way when she sat down and took a close look at all of her credit card bills. Seeing that many times she only paid the minimum, she realized that she was still paying off a pair of high-end leather heels she had purchased two years ago—a pair of shoes she hardly even wore anymore. It seemed that the credit card bill for the shoes lasted much longer than the popularity of the style.

Don't Max Out Your Credit Cards

This can be a tough one, especially if you're using your cards to pay other bills, such as grocery charges, but it's important to stay well below your limit and to keep paying them down before you charge more. The more you owe, compared to your credit limit, the lower your score.

Marilyn heard this advice from her financial advisor, who was surprised by all of the items Marilyn had purchased with her cards during her pre-financial planning shopping sprees. Luckily, Marilyn was able to pay off all of the credit card bills without repercussion, but once the accounts were settled, she was more than happy to say good-bye to the cards and avoid the risk of maxing out ever again.

A Longer Credit History Will Help Improve Your Score

As you pay off credit cards, put them away, but don't close the accounts, unless you have an excessive number of cards. If that's the case, start by closing all those retail store credit cards. This may seem as though it goes against earlier advice to ditch the cards altogether, but if you can resist the temptation of using them, keeping a few accounts open without accruing any debt is a good way of establishing strong financial stability.

Don't Open a Lot of Credit Card Accounts

This step runs along the same lines as the previous one in that it is important to maintain the accounts you may already have—as long as you keep the spending on them low or cut it out entirely—but avoid applying for new cards completely. Every time you apply for credit or for a credit card, it lowers your score. Think of it as taking too many classes in one semester. You need some in order to keep your GPA up and to graduate on time, but loading up on too many will stretch you too thin. You may have plenty of credits, but your grades will eventually start slipping—just like your credit score.

If You Are Shopping for a Mortgage or Other Loan Rate, Do It Within a Short Time Frame

In any instance where you will be filling out multiple applications, keep it short, such as thirty days, in order to minimize the effect of those multiple applications on your score. Moreover, you should check your credit report about six months in advance to give you time to repair any missteps in your credit history.

Avoid Rolling Your Cards Around to Get Better Rates

When you roll your credit cards, it lowers your credit score. I've said it before, but like financial literacy, it's always worth reinforcing: pay down your cards as quickly as possible. There is no better way to bring up that low credit rating.

If You Fall Behind on Your Payments, Stop Charging and Get Caught Up Immediately

Pile payments onto the card you were late on to pay it off as quickly as possible, but do not neglect your other card payments in the meantime. As I mentioned earlier, it can be tempting to let those payments slide, but your credit score will never improve as long as you have outstanding bills.

Check Your Credit Report Regularly

You are entitled by law to one free credit report annually from each of the three major credit-reporting agencies. To get your free report, go to www.annualcreditreport.com. You may also contact Annual Credit Report Request Service, P.O. Box 105281, Atlanta, GA 30348-5281, or by phone at (877) 322-8228. Be sure to make certain your credit reports are accurate, and correct inaccuracies immediately by contacting the credit reporting agencies directly.

Of course, credit card debt isn't the only thing that can influence your credit rating. However, many people are under the mistaken impression that something that can do a great deal of damage to a credit score is the only way out of their money problems.

BANKRUPTCY: THE WHY AND WHEREFORE

Bankruptcy. It's not a pleasant word. Yet more and more you might hear some people claiming it is the best way out of a bad financial situation. Unfortunately, bankruptcy can often do your credit more harm than good.

Bankruptcy is a negative event on your credit record. It may impede your ability to get new credit, buy a home, car, or other major purchase, rent a car, rent an apartment, obtain insurance, or even get a job. In order to discharge all of your debts in Chapter 7 of the Bankruptcy Code, you must qualify by a means test to show that you do not have adequate income to pay your bills. In Chapter 13 bankruptcy, on the other hand, you restructure to pay off some of your bills.

Keep in mind, some bills are not dischargeable in bankruptcy, such as student loans, alimony and child support in arrears, and back taxes. Bankruptcy may stay on your credit report for up to seven to ten years. It is also disruptive to families and may cause marital stress, loss of one's home, removal from schools, and emotional trauma. All in all, it is something to be avoided at all costs.

Obviously, no one wants to declare bankruptcy. It just happens. It happens as a result of unexpected health problem, job loss, or divorce. It can happen as a result of a lot of missteps, any of which might have served as a red flag that trouble was imminent.

Intoxicated on real estate—that's what one of my clients, Gail, said was the cause of her bankruptcy. She bought her "dream home" at the top of the real estate market, put zero down, and took out a mortgage. Six months later, she took $100,000 of equity out of her home to buy a condo in Las Vegas, and the following year, she took another $100,000 out of her condo in Las Vegas to buy a condo in Miami.

Two years later, the real estate market collapsed and Gail found herself upside down on all her properties. The week before she declared bankruptcy, Gail went to see her financial advisor, who sent her to see a bankruptcy attorney. Sadly, it was already too late. She was so far behind in her mortgages and credit cards that there was no time left to try to work something out.

The most frustrating aspect of this situation was that Gail, like most people, didn't consult her financial advisor *before* she made any financial decisions. As I have said in previous chapters, the time to speak with a professional is long before you find yourself at bankruptcy's door. Anytime you sign a legal document, an alarm should go off in your head saying, "Stop! I'm going to consult my financial advisor (and attorney) before I sign this." The first question you should be asking yourself and your financial consultant is, "Can I afford this major purchase?" Just because you can qualify doesn't mean you should.

Health issues are also a leading cause of bankruptcy. As of 2009, fifty million nonelderly Americans (or 18.9 percent) lacked health insurance.[1] The new health care legislation may change that, but it's still important to be aware that health costs could come out of nowhere—as with Debbie Strong.

Clients Tonya and Tom had been married for many years when Tom was diagnosed with cancer. He fought the disease with admirable valor and was in and out of the hospital many times, racking up tens of thousands of dollars in medical bills. Because of all the cancer treatments, Tom did not have the strength to work. Eventually he lost his job and then his health care. Tonya worked as an administrative assistant, but her salary could not cover all the household bills, let alone the outsized medical bills.

In the end, Tonya and Tom were forced to file for bankruptcy. Their financial situation wasn't their fault, but maybe if they had consulted with an advisor they might have been able to avoid the damaging bankruptcy. Now, when they need credit more than ever, they aren't able to obtain it.

Unexpected job loss is another leading cause of bankruptcy. Many people carry balances on their credit cards for years and are able to manage it—until they lose their jobs. In an era of downsizing, it is a common experience. Often, the earner is not able to find a similar job at an equivalent salary. The earner is unwilling to take a job at a lesser pay. However, there is now a whole cadre of "discouraged workers" who cannot find a job at *any* pay. As a result, more and more of the household expenses get added to the credit cards.

Smelling blood, the credit card companies raise their interest rates and the finance charges pile on. The non-earner rolls the credit cards to new credit cards again and again until the house of cards collapses. It's becoming an all too familiar picture in recent years.

Divorce is yet another leading cause of bankruptcy. When communication breaks down and love turns to hate, resentment, and spite, evil deeds are sometimes the result. Peggy and John were married twelve years and had three young children. When Peggy discovered that John was having an affair with Peggy's co-worker, Peggy was obviously hurt. Then she became infuriated. Out of spite, she charged thousands of dollars of jewelry and clothing on their joint credit card. John couldn't control her, so in retaliation he charged thousands of dollars on electronics and tricked out motorcycle parts. When they each refused to pay the credit card bills, it was a race to the bottom.

If this sounds like you, take a breath. Consult a collaborative divorce attorney, who will help you and your spouse speak with a counselor and arrive at a fair settlement without bankrupting both parties. It is just not worth it.

Having said all of that, there are some tips you can follow that might help to avoid bankruptcy. As with anything, there are no guarantees, but if you act quickly you stand a much better chance of saving your credit score.

Value your credit. This tip was emphasized heavily earlier in the chapter, but it bears repeating that the best way to avoid bankruptcy is to keep an eye on that credit score and to manage your debt well.

Take responsibility. It seems obvious that accepting accountability for your debt would be one of the first steps in escaping a Chapter 7, but it's amazing how many people ignore the truth until it is far too late.

Avoid charging. As mentioned earlier in the chapter, you should avoid becoming overextended on any of your credit cards. In order to do that, save up for purchases rather than putting them on your credit cards. In this way you'll keep from getting in over your head on something that you can't actually afford.

Consult your financial advisor and/or attorney. Do this *before* committing to any major purchases. If Gail had followed this advice, she may have been able to avoid her damaging bankruptcy. Furthermore, if your life circumstances change and you fall behind on your bills, consult a professional advisor immediately. It may seem like an unnecessary expense at first, but it could save you many headaches in the long run.

Finally, try to negotiate a workout settlement of repayment with your lenders rather than declaring bankruptcy. Usually, lenders are willing to help you find a way out of debt without having to turn to bankruptcy. After all, they want to get their money as much as you want to be rid of them.

With all of that said, avoiding a bankruptcy is never a guarantee, and when challenging days hit, sometimes there just isn't any way around it. Nevertheless, if you take proper precautions, there is a chance to dodge the worst of the damage.

CONTROLLING THE FALLOUT

If there is absolutely no way you can avoid bankruptcy, there are some strategies that can at least lessen the blow to your credit score. First, consult a bankruptcy attorney immediately. There is no substitute for the advice of a trusted professional. Next, use a legitimate debt-counseling service, preferably one that your attorney recommends.

Once you have your professional team lined up, learn the difference between Chapter 7 and 13 bankruptcy, and choose the one that is best for your situation. Initially they may sound similar, but, as with anything in financial planning, it all depends on your circumstances.

After you've gained more literacy on bankruptcy laws and procedures, check your credit report to ensure that the reporting agencies are accurately reporting the facts of your bankruptcy. Make sure that the debts that were included in the bankruptcy are shown as discharged and that the balances are zero. Even more importantly, know the date when your bankruptcy can be removed from your credit report, and then make sure it happens.

After bankruptcy, begin immediately to re-establish your credit. You can start by obtaining a secured or pre-paid credit card that allows you to charge only what you've prepaid. Then make sure your payment history is reported to the credit reporting agencies. Finally, have patience. Time will wash away this unpleasant experience. Remember that even though you have declared bankruptcy, you are still a good person.

Now that you've taken a frank look at your finances, devised a plan for your future, and, hopefully, started the process of eliminating debt and improving your credit score, it's time to more closely examine a key factor in building the finances you will need in order to live and thrive throughout your retirement—the power of SISTERS.

REFERENCES:

1 "Health Spending and Insurance Issues." Employee Benefit Research Institute, 2012. http://www.ebri.org/publications/benfaq/index.cfm?fa=hlthfaq10.

Chapter 7

Step Five: SISTERS
Stackable Income Streams
To Empower Retirement Security

You've heard the saying "Don't put all your eggs in one basket," right? It has never been truer than in regard to helping women plan a secure and profitable retirement.

The key to SISTERS is "stacking" your income. Chances are, a single income won't be near enough to pay for even necessities, let alone fund a comfortable retirement. So what options are there for a woman facing retirement?

The key is to continue earning throughout retirement—finding ways to create income for life. Get creative. Throughout history, women have been forced to use their ingenuity to get things done, and carving out a comfortable retirement in today's economic climate is no different. On top of any Social Security and pension money that might be coming in, you can work part time or rent out your garage as rehearsal space to a struggling band—just get three or four different streams of income flowing so that when one inevitably dries up, you don't find yourself in a dire position.

Before we get into some of those more creative options, however, let's first take a look at the many traditional methods that might be available to you.

STACKING THE ODDS

The most important retirement planning objective is to accumulate and "stack" as many diverse sources of reliable retirement income as you possibly can. For example, if you had five different sources of income in retirement that each paid you $12,000 per year, it would add up to $60,000 in annual income. How many income streams will you have in retirement? Here are some ideas for varying sources of income:

- Pensions
- Social Security
- Investments and savings
- Retirement plans, 401(k) plans and IRAs
- Part-time job
- Inheritance
- Annuities
- Home-based or small business
- Rental property
- Home equity

Stackable Income Streams To Empower Retirement Security
Pensions
Investments
Social Security
Retirement Plans
IRAs
Part-time Job
Annuities
Inheritance
Home-based or Small Business
Royalties
Rental Property
Life Insurance
Home Equity

THE THREE-LEGGED STOOL

No, this isn't some new and crazy fad in home furnishing. It is actually one of the most commonly held strategies for saving for retirement. In general, the basic retirement planning methods have traditionally included three sources of income: a pension, Social Security, and income from investments. This was often called "the three-legged stool," and it was believed that these three "legs" would provide enough income to support you in retirement. Let's take them one at a time.

Pensions

A pension is a retirement income benefit provided by an employer to the employee. It is a defined benefit amount that is paid out to the employee in retirement based on a formula of your pay grade and length of service, among other factors. This is why it is called a defined benefit plan. Every year, the employer has the responsibility to set aside a defined amount of money for the employee for retirement.

Pensions have worked well in the past for many types of workers, including teachers, government employees, politicians, military personnel, union workers, engineers and corporate executives, to name a few. They have proven to be a strong source of income for many who are in retirement now. However, less than half the American workforce receives a pension. According to the Social Security "Fact Sheet," as of 2006, 52 percent of the workforce had no private pension coverage.[1] For freelancers such as Debbie Strong, pensions have never even been an option.

Moreover, pensions are a drag on corporate (or government) balance sheets, and work against a company's earnings. Therefore, employers are looking to gradually reduce or eliminate their responsibility to provide defined benefit (DB) retirement income to employees. By the time someone like Sara Strong is reaching retirement age, pensions may be a thing of the past.

According to Social Security, "the percentage of workers covered by a traditional defined benefit pension plan has been steadily declining over the past 25 years."[2] In fact, the proportion of private workers covered by a defined benefit pension fell from 38 percent to 20 percent.[3]

A 2010 retirement survey by Wells Fargo showed that those who expected to receive defined benefit pensions were highest in the near-retirees, with each subsequent generation becoming less and less sure of collecting such benefits: "59% of 60-somethings, 55% of 50-somethings, 36% of 40-somethings, 32% of 30-somethings, and 27% of 20-somethings."[4]

As you can see, while pensions may have once been a strong source of retirement income, more and more retirees, women in particular, must look to other sources to help fund their later years.

Social Security

The second leg of retirement income is Social Security. According to Social Security's 2006 Fact Sheet,[5] nine out of ten individuals age 65 and older received Social Security benefits. These benefits represented 41 percent of the income of the elderly. Among those receiving benefits, 54 percent of married couples and 74 percent of unmarried persons received 50 percent or more of their income from Social Security. And among these same elderly beneficiaries, 21 percent of married couples and about 43 percent of unmarried persons relied on Social Security for 90 percent or more of their income.

For women, Social Security is an especially important source of income. Nearly 60 percent of the people receiving Social Security benefits are women.[6] However, as pointed out in earlier chapters, because women have historically earned about three-fourths of what men earn, and because women have left the workforce for child care and other purposes, women's Social Security earnings are, on average, about three-fourths of men's (77 percent).[7] Even worse, with Social Security being threatened by lack of funding, it is expected to be exhausted in 2041.[8]

Income from Investments

Let's look at the third leg of expected retirement income, which is income from investments. Investments are also called financial assets or securities. Securities convey value to the owner. For retirement purposes we would also like to derive income from our investments. For income, we might invest in Treasury bills (also called T-bills), money market funds, CDs (certificates of deposit) or bonds (also called fixed income).

Another approach is to try to grow our investments (also known as capital appreciation, gains or profits) and then periodically use some of the profits to support our retirement lifestyle. A good way to do this is to invest in stocks (also called equities). Dividend-paying stocks may go up in value over time and also provide some income from the dividends they pay out quarterly. Keep in mind stocks may go up or down in value.

An easy way for the small investor to get started is through mutual funds. Mutual funds pool your money with other investors' money into a common mutual fund, which allows the mutual fund company to keep the initial investment and fees relatively low, and to hire a professional investment manager to manage your investment.

MAKING YOUR 401(k) WORK FOR YOU

In trying to find different ways to create stackable income, the 401(k) can still be one of your best bets—if you manage it correctly. Luckily, there are some relatively simple steps to making the most of that 401(k) plan.

Maximize Your Contributions

This is a great way to save for retirement. Put in at least 10 percent if you can. Just as I discussed in an earlier chapter, it is a good way of paying yourself first.

Use Any Raise to Increase Your Contributions, Not Your Spending

Whenever we earn a pay bump, the natural instinct is to go out and buy things—a new house, a better car, or some stylish clothes, for example. However, if you really want to build your 401(k), start contributing that extra money to a good cause—your retirement.

Know Your Investment Options

What is your menu of mutual funds from which to choose? Look up the mutual funds on the 401(k) plan's website or on the mutual fund's website, or on the financial website of your choice, such as Yahoo! Finance. What are the mutual funds' investment objectives—growth, income, safety? How have the mutual funds performed? Do a little homework—it all comes back to understanding your personal finances and what will work best for *your* situation.

Create a Diversified Asset Allocation

The easiest way to do this is with an asset allocation fund, the process of balancing your investments between various asset classes in order to diversify your investments between different categories of investments, such as stocks, bonds, and cash. A variation on the asset allocation fund is the retirement lifestyle fund, which gradually changes the asset allocation to become increasingly more conservative as you get older.

Meet with Your Financial Advisor

Make an appointment to see your investment representative in order to discuss your investment options and your asset allocation.

Track Your 401(k) Account Quarterly

Put your quarterly statements in a notebook; this is a great exercise to include as part of the log you have hopefully started. Watch your balance grow. If it's not growing, that's a sign that perhaps you need to adjust your asset allocation.

Never Borrow from Your 401(k) or Withdraw from Your IRA

If you are under 59½, you will have to pay a 10 percent penalty and income taxes on the withdrawal from your IRA if you do not repay the amount withdrawn within sixty days. If you take a loan from your 401(k), you will also have to pay the loan back with after-tax dollars, which will be taxed again when you do retire and distribute the funds. It is a strategy that does not make good financial sense.

In particular, do not borrow from your 401(k) for personal indulgences, such as a new kitchen, a vacation, or even a new car. These are expenditures that should be planned for out of your regular budget. If you cannot afford them, either you are living above your means, not saving enough, or need to take a hard look at your current earning situation and possibly consider a better-paying job.

Do Not Take Money Out of Your 401(k) Plan for College for Your Children

It's tempting, especially for women such as Wanda Strong, who worries about paying her children's tuition, but if you follow such a strategy, you will not have enough time to recoup your savings before retirement. It would be better to send your child to a state school or community college, or let your son or daughter take out student loans, as long as they are reasonable in amount. As unpalatable as that may sound, your child has a lifetime of earning potential to pay back the loans. You do not.

No 401(k) Left Behind

If you change jobs, do not leave your 401(k) account behind. No one will watch it for you, and you will be less likely to watch it once you leave that job. Consider rolling it into your new 401(k) plan or a rollover IRA, which would probably give you more investment choices.

Learn About Your Investments

Your 401(k) plan may be your most important savings vehicle. Spend some time to learn about investments. I cannot emphasize this point enough—go to the library and become financially literate.

THE POWER OF AN IRA

Most people are now familiar with the individual retirement account (IRA). These are tax-deferred retirement savings accounts. You could contribute $5500 to your IRA in 2014, fully deductible if neither individual nor spouse is a participant in another plan, or $6500 if you are over 50 years of age, as a "catch-up contribution" to help those nearing retirement save more. Contributions may have full or partial tax-deductibility if you are single and have modified adjusted gross income (MAGI) of less than $60,000 to $70,000; or married, filing jointly and covered by a work plan, with MAGI of less than $96,000 to $116,000. Consult your CPA for more specifics.

IRAs are "self-directed," which means that you are responsible for choosing your own investments. You have a broad range of investments to choose from when investing in your IRA, including stocks, bonds, mutual funds, cash, ETFs, managed accounts, and specialized commodity investments. This is one advantage to rolling over your 401(k) into an IRA.

As I just mentioned, many people neglect to bring their outdated retirement accounts with them when they change jobs or move. They leave behind 401(k) and IRA accounts like so many "forgotten children." However, it is not conducive to good management of your retirement savings to leave your accounts behind unattended like this. A better approach may be to consolidate all of your accounts in one place so that you can keep a watchful eye on them.

Another option is the Roth IRA, which is different from the traditional IRA in that when you contribute to a Roth IRA, you do so with after-tax dollars. That means you have already paid income taxes on the money you use to contribute to the Roth IRA, so you do not get a tax deduction. However, with the Roth, all earnings grow tax-free.

The contributions to the traditional IRA may or may not be tax-deductible, depending on your income, and the earnings are tax-deferred, which means you will be taxed on them when you withdraw from the traditional IRA. You must qualify for a Roth IRA by having an adjusted gross income that is lower than a specific amount (in 2014, it was $114,000 to $129,000 for singles and $181,000 to $191,000 for married couples).

The benefit of the Roth is that all earnings grow tax-free. Let's say you put in $5,000 in a mutual fund inside a Roth IRA and it grows to $7,000. The $2,000 in earnings is tax-free growth. When you reach retirement and need to take money out of your retirement accounts to live on, the withdrawals are tax-free. Nonetheless, perhaps the most appealing feature of a Roth IRA is that if you don't need the money, you never have to take it out of your account. You can just keep letting it grow forever. This can be extremely beneficial if you leave the Roth IRA to a child or grandchild.

By contrast, with the traditional or rollover IRA, when you reach age 70½, you must withdraw a percentage of your IRA account value, because the IRS wants to tax you on it. These withdrawals are known as Required Minimum Distributions (RMDs). The amount you must take out and pay taxes on is based on your life expectancy as required by the IRS schedule.

As you can see, there are many viable traditional options for creating several "stacked" streams of income throughout your retirement. The important thing to take from all of this is that you should put *several* of these income streams into place. When I worked in the jewelry industry, most people specialized in only one area, such as diamonds, diamond cutting, colored stones, retail, or appraisal and gemology. I, on the other hand, had taught myself all of those skills, because I felt like it was something I needed to know in order for my business to be successful. I was a bit unusual in that regard, but that is the kind of broad reach women should have when devising their retirement plan.

We've talked about Part One of the SISTERS model, and I've shared with you the secret of stacking several streams of income. But I've barely scraped the surface of investments, which should be a fundamental part of every woman's strategy. If you invest wisely, your investments can produce a steady income stream to help fund your retirement. So let's move into Part Two of SISTERS: creating income from investments.

REFERENCES:

1 "Fact Sheet." USA Social Security Administration, 2012. www.ssa.gov/pressoffice/factsheets/colafacts2012.pdf.

2 Butrica, Barbara A., Howard M. Iams, Karen E. Smith, and Eric J. Toder, "The Disappearing Defined Benefit Pension and Its Potential Impact on the Retirement Incomes of Baby Boomers"; Social Security Bulletin, Vol. 69, No. 3, 2009. http://www.ssa.gov/policy/docs/ssb/v69n3/v69n3p1.pdf.

3 Barbara A. Butrica et al., "The Disappearing Defined Benefit Pension and Its Potential Impact on the Retirement Incomes of Baby Boomers."

4 2010 Wells Fargo Retirement Study.

5 www.ssa.gov/pressoffice/factsheets/colafacts2012.pdf.

6 "What Every Woman Should Know." Social Security Administration.

7 Social Security's Annual Statistical Supplement, 2010.

8 Social Security Administration's 2005 Annual Report to Congress.

Chapter 8

Creating Income from Investments

My mother was thirty-one when her mother passed away, leaving her a small inheritance. She went to the library and researched investment stocks with the help of the librarian. After much investigation or "due diligence," she bought several high-quality dividend stocks and watched them closely. The stocks grew in value over time, and split several times, multiplying the share count. When my mother retired, the dividends from those stocks amounted to several thousand dollars per quarter, becoming an important source of her retirement income.

My mother had created her first stackable income stream.

This is just one example of how investments can produce income. Investments are a fundamental part of the SISTERS model—an excellent way to create a stackable income stream that, if managed wisely, can produce big results.

Investments come in many forms. These may include financial investments such as certificates of deposits (CDs), stocks, bonds, mutual funds, and annuities, or real estate, such as your home.

Because of the housing bubble, real estate has been problematic in recent years. Many people bought at the top of the market, with little or no money down. In 2013—five years after the bubble burst—millions of homeowners remained "underwater." A 2012 study showed that fifty- to fifty-four-year-old homeowners are generally 30 percent underwater, and 10 percent of these are significantly behind on their mortgages.[1]

Those who have owned their homes for a longer period of time may have more equity, or ownership, in their homes. In this case, a home may be a safety net for a retiree, especially if it is paid off by the time one retires. But because of the changes in the laws regarding mortgages, home affordability may now be out of reach for many.

An advantage to financial investments is that they can be quite affordable, with minimum investments in mutual funds starting anywhere between $250 and $1,000. This is an excellent option for women who want to start small, as you may be able to build up your investments with as little as $50 per month.

In this chapter, I will provide an overview of the financial products and instruments I most often recommend to my clients, including CDs, stocks, bonds, dividends-paying investments, mutual funds, and ETFs. In Chapter 9, we will take a more in-depth look at determining which investments are right for you, as well as what to do once you have them. We'll also talk about where annuities fit into your investment portfolio.

First, let's begin by defining our terms.

CERTIFICATES OF DEPOSIT (CDs)

Most of us have owned a CD at one time or another. It is a *certificate* (piece of paper) that verifies that you made a *deposit* of money, usually in $1,000 increments, with the financial institution (bank or investment firm). CDs are backed by the government through FDIC insurance up to a limit, which was permanently increased to $250,000 in 2011.[2]

The investor holds the CD for a certain period of time and receives a specified *interest* income. The interest income, or interest, is fixed in the CD contract at the inception and never changes. At maturity—the end of the specified holding period—the CD matures and the investor receives his or her $1,000 principal back, plus any interest due.

STOCKS = EQUITIES

Common stocks are also called *equities* because they convey ownership in companies. When you buy a stock, you become an owner of the company—however small. Typically an investor buys 100 shares or more at a time, which is known as a *round lot*. A round lot is 100 shares. Anything fewer than 100 shares is called an *odd lot*. It is generally believed that inexperienced investors buy odd lot quantities of fewer than 100 shares.

When you buy a stock, you become a *stockholder* or *shareholder*. You have equity or ownership in the company. (Similarly, when you buy a home, you have equity or ownership in the home.) As an owner of the company, you have certain rights. You have the right to vote for the board of directors. You have the right to maintain your same percentage ownership in the company—that is, the company cannot dilute your ownership through restructuring. And you have the right to receive dividends if the company pays them.

Dividends are payments that the company pays to shareholders for the use of their investment dollars and to encourage them to keep their money invested in the company. They are usually paid in cash but may also be paid in stock or extra shares of the company. Dividends have historically been an excellent way to create cash flow (income) in retirement. As of this writing in 2014, qualified dividends have tax advantages in that they are taxed at your long-term capital gains rate, which is 0 percent if you are in the 10 and 15 percent tax brackets, 15 percent if you are in the 25 through 35 percent tax brackets, and 20 percent if you are in the 39.6 percent tax bracket.[3] The capital gains rate is usually lower than your income tax bracket. That makes dividend-paying stocks very attractive—especially for those in higher tax brackets.

One way to compare dividend-paying stocks is to compare their dividend yields, or how much they pay out in dividends as a percentage of their current share price.

The dividend yield for a company's stock is the ratio of the dividends paid out by the company each year per share as a percentage of (divided by) the share's current market price.

$$\text{DIVIDEND YIELD} = \frac{\text{ANNUAL DIVIDEND}}{\text{CURRENT SHARE PRICE}}$$

(Source: CEFconnect.com)

Of course, you also want to compare other factors such as the company's history of paying dividends, the earnings per share (EPS), or how much the company is earning, and the price to earnings "multiple," or P/E, which tells you how expensive the stock is relative to its peers.

$$\text{Earnings Per Share (EPS)} = \frac{\text{Total Earnings of the Company}}{\text{Number of Shares Outstanding}}$$

$$\text{Price to Earnings Multiple (P/E)} = \frac{\text{Share Price}}{\text{Earnings Per Share}}$$

BONDS = FIXED INCOME

Bonds are another excellent source of income. All bonds pay out a stated interest rate. That rate is *fixed* (locked in) in the original bond contract when the bonds are first *issued*, or offered for sale. Since the interest rate (also called the "coupon") is fixed, it never changes for the duration of the bond. The investor receives a fixed income for the life of the bond, which is why bonds are also called *fixed income.*

Bonds pay interest regularly—usually semiannually, although some pay monthly—and are generally not as volatile as the stock market. Therefore, bonds may be a good choice for those who want income and some degree of safety. One word of caution: bonds come in a wide range of investment qualities. If you are new to bond investing, be sure your bonds are high quality or in a diversified portfolio of bonds, such as a bond mutual fund.

Bonds are issued in $1,000 increments for corporate bonds and $5,000 for municipal bonds. This is known as the *face amount* or *par value*. The face amount or par value is the dollar amount stated on the bond certificate at which the bond is issued and off of which the interest amount is calculated. For example, a bond with a face amount or par value of $1,000 and a coupon, or interest rate, of 6 percent pays bondholders $60 per year.[4]

The par value or face amount is the dollar amount stated on the bond certificate at which the bond is issued, and off of which the interest amount is calculated.

$1,000 BOND x 6.00% COUPON = $60 PER YEAR INTEREST INCOME
or
$1,000 x (0.06) = $60

(Source: Downs, John, and Jordan Elliot Goodman, Barron's Dictionary of Finance and Investment Terms)

Everything You Ever Wanted to Know About Bonds

Bonds may be *issued*, or offered for sale, by the U.S. government, state governments, and local municipalities, such as counties or cities. Governments issue bonds to raise money for public works such as roads, schools, sewers, and general operations.

Corporations like IBM and GE also issue bonds. They sell bonds to raise money to cover the cost of capital expenditures such as buildings, equipment, and the cost of doing business.

Bonds are backed by the issuer. That means the issuer is responsible to pay the interest regularly and to pay back the bondholder when the bond matures. If the bond is issued by the U.S. government, then the U.S. government is responsible to pay the bondholder. If the bond is issued by the city of Chicago, then the city of Chicago is responsible to pay the bondholder. Similarly, if a corporation such as GE or IBM issues the bond, then that corporation is responsible to pay the bond-holder.

Bonds are rated for credit quality. Just as individuals have a FICO score, bonds have a credit rating. There are credit rating agencies, such as Moody's and Standard & Poor's (S&P), that rate the credit quality of state and local governments as well as corporations, and assess their ability to repay the bond investor.

Until recently, the U.S. government had a AAA (tri-ple A) rating, the highest rating available. In 2011, S&P downgraded the credit rating of the U.S. government to AA+. Still, the U.S. government is generally considered the safest creditor in the world, which is why foreigners, pensions, mutual funds, and individuals buy U.S. gov-ernment bonds.

Credit ratings are assigned to the issuer based on the financial strength of the issuer's balance sheet ("check-book"). Another factor is how much income or cash flow the issuer has to repay the bondholders.

Here is a chart of credit ratings.

STANDARD & POOR'S	MOODY'S	COMMENTS
		Investment Grade Ratings
AAA	Aaa	Highest possible credit rating—principal and interest payments considered very secure.
AA	Aa	High quality—differs from highest rating only in the degree of protection offered to bondholders.
A	A	Good ability to pay interest and principal—more susceptible to adverse effects due to changing conditions.
BBB	Baa	Adequate ability to make principal and interest payments—adverse conditions are more likely to affect ability to service debt.
		Speculative ratings
BB	Ba	Issuer faces ongoing uncertainties or exposure to adverse business or economic conditions.
B	B	Greater vulnerability to default, but currently meeting debt-service requirements.
C	Caa	Current identifiable risks of default—in some cases, bonds may already be in default.
D	C	Bonds in default[5]

Any bond rated BBB or higher by S&P, or Baa or higher by Moody's, is considered an investment-grade bond. Any bond rated BB or lower by S&Ps, or Ba or

> **"Default"** is the failure of a bond issuer to pay interest or principal when due.
>
> *(Source: "A Guide to Investing in High-Yield Bonds," Wells Fargo Advisors)*

lower by Moody's, is considered non-investment grade and speculative. It is also called a junk bond or a high-yield bond.

The higher the credit quality, the safer the bond, and the less interest income the issuer must pay out to attract investors. That's why U.S. government bonds pay less interest than other types of bonds—they're safer.

The lower the credit quality, the greater the risk that the bond investor will not get paid back principal and interest. Therefore, lower-quality bond issuers have to pay a higher interest rate to attract bond investors. High-yield or junk bonds are lower-quality bonds that put the bond investor's money at risk. Junk bonds pay higher interest income to investors, but they are risky.

Here is a hypothetical relationship of corporate bond interest rates to credit quality.

S&P Credit Rating	Hypothetical Interest Rate Percent (%) for Corporate Bond
AAA	5
AA	5 ½
A	6
BBB	6 ½
BB	8 ½
B	10
C	12
D	Default

Note: This illustration of yield to credit quality relationships is hypothetical. For actual rates by credit rating, consult a daily financial newspaper, such as The Wall Street Journal.

Municipalities, such as states, counties, and cities, also issue bonds. Most of these bonds are tax-exempt. They are triple tax-free to investors who are residents of the state in which the bonds are issued. That means that the bondholder pays no federal, state, or local income taxes on the interest they receive. This is very beneficial to those who are in a high tax bracket but may not benefit those in a low tax bracket—as we discussed in Chapter 4.

If you're in a lower tax bracket, corporate bonds may be a better choice. Depending on the economic environment, it may be possible to get a higher interest rate (or *yield*) on municipal bonds than corporate bonds of the same quality, after taxation is taken into account.

Bonds are generally considered safer than preferred stocks or common stocks. If the company *defaults*, or fails to make an interest or principal payment to bondholders, it is considered *bankrupt*. In bankruptcy, bondholders have highest rights to the *residual assets* of

---

- "Current yield" is the annual return on the dollar amount paid for a bond.

- "Yield to maturity" is the rate of return the investor earned from payments of principal and interest, with interest compounded semiannually at the stated yield, until maturity date.

- Yield to maturity takes into account the amount of the premium or discount, if any, and the time value of the investment.

(Source: "Tax-exempt Municipal Bonds," Wells Fargo Advisors)

---

the company. *Residual assets* are anything of value that is left after a company goes bankrupt. There may be little or nothing left for stakeholders after the company goes bankrupt. Sometimes it amounts to pennies on the dollar, and often it is nothing.

If there are any residual assets, the bondholders get paid their principal back first, then the preferred stockholders get paid back, and then the common shareholders get paid back, in that order.

The fastest, easiest, and most cost-effective way for the small investor to invest in bonds is through a mutual fund or exchange-traded fund (ETF) that invests in bonds.

> High quality bonds may be a good investment choice if you want retirement income with some degree of safety. If you are in a high tax bracket, you may want to consider municipal bonds. If you are in a low tax bracket, you may want to consider corporate bonds. Be sure to select the bond with the credit rating that is right for you.

PREFERRED STOCKS

Preferred stocks are a hybrid between stocks and bonds. They are fixed-income securities with attributes of both equity (stocks) and fixed income (bonds).[6] Preferred stocks are typically issued in $25 increments (the *par value*) and trade on the New York Stock Exchange. Preferred stocks pay out a dividend that is usually higher than the dividend on the common stock or the interest paid out on the bond issued by the same company.

In general, the bond is considered the safest, the preferred stock is the next safest, and the common stock the riskiest of three if the company goes into bankruptcy and liquidates.

Although the preferred stock receives a higher dividend than the stock, it has limited growth potential should the market go up. The stock can appreciate in price, whereas the preferred stock usually trades in a narrow price range. Preferred stockholders don't have the same voting rights as the common stockholders—for example, the right to vote for the board of directors.

Preferred stocks come in two types: cumulative and non-cumulative. If a company misses a dividend payment, cumulative preferred stockholders must be paid all dividends in arrears before common stockholders get paid any dividends. Non-cumulative preferreds do not have this protective feature, so cumulative preferreds have an extra safety feature for investors.

Preferred stocks have traditionally been used by investors looking for higher income with a moderate degree of safety. This may have appeal for retirees living on a fixed income.

Below is a chart that shows a simplified, hypothetical relationship between the stock, the bond, and the preferred stock issued by the ABC Company.

ABC Company Rating	Hypothetical Interest or Dividend Percent (%)
Bond	5%
Preferred Stock	6.5%
Common Stock	2.75%

This chart is simplified, but it shows that each security has its own rate at which it pays out to investors. If the company liquidates, the bondholders will get paid first, the preferred shareholders will get paid second, and the common stockholders will get paid last.

> A **"security"** is another word for an investment instrument, such as a stock or a bond. Financial securities are financial instruments.
>
> *(Source: SEC: Investor.Gov)*

MUTUAL FUNDS

Odd as it may seem now, in the early days of the market, it was difficult for small investors to get into the stock market with a small amount of money. In 1924, some professors at Massachusetts Institute of Technology (MIT) decided to pool their funds into one *mutual fund* to have more money to access the markets. This was the Massachusetts Investors Trust. A contract was drawn up, and everyone in the mutual fund had an *undivided*, or equivalent and fair, interest in the fund, according to how much he or she invested. That was the first mutual fund. It was quite an innovation![7]

Now mutual funds are ubiquitous, being the investment choice of 401(k) plans and IRAs. Small investors can get into mutual funds with as little as $500 or $50 per month. Mutual funds invest in many types of financial investments, such as stocks, bonds, and money market instruments. They may strive to replicate market indexes, such as the S&P 500 Index, a measure of the broad market. They may have an investment objective, such as "growth," in which case they try to attain a higher return on the investor's invested dollars; or, "income," in which case they try to invest in bonds or other instruments that will provide more income. Or they may have a "balanced" objective, in which case they will strive for a balance between growth and income. Mutual funds may also invest in sectors of the economy, such as utilities or technology.

Mutual funds have some distinct advantages. They provide professional management, diversification, convenience, low investment requirements, and attainable investment fees. Shares of the mutual funds are always redeemed by the mutual fund company, so they are easy for small investors to buy and sell.

Mutual funds are not entirely transparent in what they hold in their portfolios. They report to mutual-fund holders only quarterly. However, you can generally see their top ten holdings on their fact sheets, which gives you a flavor for their investment style. If you go on the mutual-fund website, you may see an updated explanation of their holdings. All mutual funds, even no-load funds, have embedded management fees. These fees cover the cost of the investment manager, the operations of the mutual fund company, and the marketing of the mutual funds. They may also have a sales charge, which is how the financial advisor gets paid.

Mutual funds may or may not be tax-efficient. Still, mutual funds provide potentially great opportunities for small or novice investors to get started in the market for retirement or college planning.

> A mutual fund is a type of investment company that pools money from many investors and invests the money in stocks, bonds, money-market instruments, other securities, or even cash.
>
> (Source: www.sec.gov/answers/mutfunds.com)

EXCHANGE-TRADED FUNDS

An exchange-traded fund (ETF) is similar to a mutual fund in that it is a portfolio of investments, such as stocks or bonds. It differs from a mutual fund in that it trades on the stock exchange like a stock, all day long. Investors can buy and sell ETFs any moment of the trading day. By contrast, mutual funds trade once per day, at the end of the day. Most ETFs track an index (such as the S&P 500), or are focused on a particular sector.

ETFs vary greatly in structure and risk. They may have passive or active management. They may employ leverage, invest in futures and derivatives markets, or short the market, which means they seek to deliver the opposite of the performance of the index or benchmark they track. They may also have "tracking error," which means that they do not track or mimic the underlying index as well as expected.[8]

An exchange-traded fund (ETF) is a fund of underlying investments that trades on an exchange like a stock. Most ETFs track an index or are focused on a particular sector.

(Source: Etfconnect.com)

Consider this a "survey" of the many investment options available to you. However, as any smart woman knows, knowledge is only the beginning. Without accompanying action, knowledge won't do you any good. In the next chapter, I want to show you *how* investments can function as stackable income streams to help fund your retirement.

REFERENCES:

1 Glink, Ilyce. "Nearly Half of Younger Homeowners Are 'Underwater.'" MoneyWatch; 2012 CBS Interactive, Inc. http://www.cbsnews.com/8301-505145_162-57498459/nearly-half-of-younger-homeowners-are-underwater/.

2 https://www.wellsfargo.com/savings_cds/fdic.

3 Wells Fargo Advisors: "Understanding the American Taxpayer Relief Act of 2012." January 2013, p 2.

4 Downes, John and Jordan Elliot Goodman. Barron's Dictionary of Finance and Investment Terms.

5 Chart courtesy of "Corporate Bonds," Wells Fargo Advisors.

6 Wells Fargo Advisors, "Hybrid Securities."

7 "Unmatched History: We Invented the Mutual Fund," MFS Investment Management. https://www.mfs.com/wps/FileServerServlet?articleId=templatedata/internet/file/data/sales_tools/mfsp_story_bro&servletCommand=default.

8 "A Guide to Investing in Exchange-traded Funds: What You Should Know Before You Buy," Wells Fargo Advisors.

Chapter 9

Savvy Strategies
for the Stock Market

Now that we have discussed specific financial products and instruments, I want to guide you through the
next stage of the process. It is time to decide which
investments are right for you and how to allocate your
assets. As an investor, it is your responsibility to not
only choose the right investments but also to measure
their success. To adequately protect your retirement,
you must strategize, measure, and monitor, every step
of the way.

DETERMINING YOUR TOTAL RETURN

It is important to periodically measure your progress and
success as an investor. You may need a metric by which
to compare investments and measure your success. *Total*

return is the combined value of the interest or dividend income the investment pays, plus the change in the dollar value of the investment, which may be positive or negative. Investments may go up or down in the market.

Here is an example. Let's say you buy 100 shares of ABC Company at $50 and it pays a $1 quarterly dividend ($4 annually). You sell the stock one year later for $55. What was your total return?

The stock went up 5 points ($5 of *capital appreciation*), plus you earned $4 in dividends for the year. Your total return would be:

$$\$50 \rightarrow \$55 \quad = \quad \underline{\$5 \text{ Capital Appreciation plus}}$$
$$\$1 \times 4 \text{ quarterly dividends} \quad = \quad \underline{\$4 \text{ Dividend Income}}$$
$$\text{Total Return} \quad = \quad \$9$$

So what percent did your investment return in total? The *total return percent* equals your total return in dollars divided by your original investment in dollars.

$$\text{Total Return Percent} \quad = \quad \underline{\text{Total Return divided by}}$$
$$\text{Original Investment}$$

$$18\% \quad = \quad \underline{\$9 \text{ divided by}}$$
$$\$50$$

> - **Total return** is the combined value of the interest or divided income the investment pays, plus the change in the dollar value of the investment, which may be positive or negative.
>
> - **Capital** is another word for money or invested principal. Capital appreciation occurs when your investments go up in value. Capital depreciation occurs when your investments go down in value.

It is also necessary to consider the effect of taxes on your investments. How much do you earn after you pay taxes on your profits? We have already discussed the differences between taxable and tax-free bonds. The goal is to maximize the after-tax return.

It is a good idea to understand how current tax law applies to your investments and the timing of when you buy and sell investments. For example, under current tax law (2014), if you sell an investment that you held less than one year, your profits are subject to *short-term capital gains* taxes, which are equal to your current income tax bracket.

If you are in the 35 percent tax bracket, short-term gains are taxed at 35 percent. If you sell an investment that you held more than one year, your profits are subject to *long-term capital gains*, which are lower than your current income tax bracket. If you are in the 25 to 35 percent tax bracket, your profits will be taxed at the long-term capital gains rate of 15 percent (in 2014). Taxation should not be the sole factor in whether to buy or sell an investment. Buy and sell on fundamentals. Learn the rules of taxation so you can be smart about taxes.

Estate taxes can also greatly affect wealth transfer and the amount of money your estate keeps. Consult an estate-planning attorney to get professional advice on how to best structure your estate to minimize taxes and optimize your investments.

STRATEGIES TO HELP CREATE WEALTH IN THE STOCK MARKET

Before we can discuss stock market strategies, it is necessary to discuss your goals, investment objectives, and time horizon. For this discussion, we will assume that your goal is to invest for retirement. Your investment objective might be "growth," in which case you would want to grow your investments over time.

Or, your objective might be "growth and income." In that case, you might want to allocate some of your investment funds into dividend paying stocks, or divide your funds partly into growth stocks and partly into safer instruments like bonds or CDs.

Or, your objective might be "income," in which case you may want to allocate your investment funds to income-producing investments, such as bonds, preferred stocks, and CDs.

It is also necessary to define your *risk tolerance*. Risk tolerance is the amount of risk you are willing to take in any investment. Ask yourself, on a scale of 1 to 5, 1 being cash and 5 being speculative, how much risk are you willing to take?

- If your risk tolerance is 1, you should probably stick with CDs.
- If your risk tolerance is 2, you may want to invest in CDs, bonds, and guaranteed investments, such as fixed annuities.
- If your risk tolerance is 3, you may consider investing conservatively in a mixture of stocks, bonds, and mutual funds.
- If your risk tolerance is 4, you are probably comfortable investing in a variety of investments, including stocks, bonds, and mutual funds. You may also allocate a higher percentage of your assets to stocks than to CDs or bonds.
- If your risk tolerance is 5, you are comfortable with riskier investments, such as stocks, and can tolerate more volatility in price movements.

ASSET ALLOCATION

The goal in investing is to create a portfolio that will give you the most total return with the least amount of risk. This is known as the *optimal portfolio*. This is accomplished in two steps: First, decide on an asset allocation that you are comfortable with. Second, select individual securities (stocks, bonds, mutual funds, etc.)

> The optimal portfolio is the one that will give you the most total return with the least amount of risk.

that will help you meet your goals and objectives within your risk tolerance.

Asset allocation is the process of balancing your investments between various asset classes. This is not about individual stock selection; it is how you diversify your investments between different categories of investments, such as stocks, bonds, and cash. For example, what percent of your investment dollars do you put in stocks, bonds, cash, real estate, precious metals, etc.? This is your mix of investments.

Asset allocation has been shown to be a key determinant of your investment success. According to *Financial Analysts Journal*, asset allocation accounts for 91.5 percent of your portfolio's success, while individual security selection accounts for just 4.6 percent of your portfolio's return, and market timing just 2.2 percent.[1] This means that the primary factor in your portfolio's success depends on how you allocate or divide your portfolio between asset classes.

One historical piece of wisdom has been to use your

age as a guide for how much you should have in bonds, with the balance in stocks. For example, if you are age fifty-two, you would want to have 52 percent of your portfolio in bonds, 48 percent in stocks.

Some take issue with this formula. Writing in *The Wall Street Journal,* James B. Stewart feels that this age/allocation formula is "grossly simplistic at best and dangerous at worst. Stocks are more risky (and volatile) than bonds over most periods. But as long as your time horizon is ten years or longer (which should include everyone up to age seventy-five based on life expectancies), the risk in owning stocks seems exaggerated. The average return for all ten-year periods was an annualized gain of nearly 10 percent and the best returns were over 18 percent. Even in the last decade (2000 to 2010), with two market crashes, returns on stocks were essentially flat. In other words, the percentage of savings in stocks isn't likely to decline by much, let alone vanish, over ten years or more. No matter what a person's age, an asset-allocation plan has to start with an investor's net worth, then balance expected returns with expected needs, and take into account risk tolerance. Everyone's circumstances will be different."[2]

In periods of low interest rates, retirees living on a fixed income who have a portfolio holding predominantly bonds will have a difficult time eking out a living on the paltry interest income from low-yielding CDs and bonds. This almost forces them out of CDs and bonds into riskier assets, such as stocks.

Target-date funds are mutual funds whose allocations gradually decrease exposure to stocks and increase the bond weightings in the portfolio as one gets closer to retirement. These have experienced popularity in 401(k) and other plans. However, though they were created to protect investors with turnkey asset allocations, "these funds performed much worse than expected during the financial crisis," according to an article in *The Wall Street Journal*.[3] There is no perfect investment. The wise investor will keep a close eye on her investments, and consult a financial advisor for questions about asset allocation.

Like most markets, the bond market is cyclical. Bonds do not perform well in times of rising interest rates. So when the Federal Reserve is raising rates, the price of bonds may erode. (If the bonds are held to maturity, they will mature at par and the investor will receive the full face value of the bond.) Also, bonds generally do not perform well in times of high inflation, as the interest on the bonds may not keep pace with inflation.

Another historical standard of prudence in asset allocation is to keep 60 percent in stocks and 40 percent in bonds and cash. The idea here is that the slight overweighting in stocks will help outpace inflation.

Still another approach to asset allocation is to

determine if you are a growth investor, a growth and income investor, or strictly an income investor. Growth investing is suitable for young people with a long investment horizon, or those who have a strong tolerance for volatility and risk. A growth investor would be more likely to invest in equities (stocks) of large-, mid- and small-sized companies, as well as some international stocks.

A growth and income investor seeks growth for part of the portfolio and income for part of the portfolio. Dividend-paying stocks offer current income from the dividends and opportunity for growth in the stock market, and are usually comprised of larger, better-capitalized companies. Growth and income investors might also consider a well-diversified mutual fund, made up of some stocks and some bonds.

Income investors who seek only income often consider bonds, preferred stocks, and other interest-bearing instruments, such as REITs, or real estate investment trusts. Income investors do not expect market growth of their investments, so they need to have adequate assets to live on the relatively safer but lower yields of income investments such as bonds.

The correct choice of asset allocation is the one that will help you achieve your financial goals and meet your objectives with the least amount of risk and volatility. This is where an experienced financial advisor can help.

Financial advisors help clients determine which asset allocation is best for them, and understand the ramifications of these important choices.

SECURITY SELECTION AND DIVERSIFICATION

The second part of creating an optimal portfolio is security selection. This is where you choose the individual stocks, bonds, and/or mutual funds that will go into your portfolio. The key to security selection is *diversification*. Diversification means not putting all your eggs in one basket. To diversify means to include a broad number and range of securities in your portfolio that have different characteristics and perform differently from each

> My client Carolyn and I sat in my office as we reviewed her portfolio one day. She said, "Even in the worst of the recession, I noticed that my portfolio never really went down much because if one part of the portfolio was down, there was another part of the portfolio that was up." **That's diversification.**

other under different market conditions. In other words, you want one part of your portfolio to zig, while another part zags.

If you've never invested in the stock market, start by giving yourself permission to make mistakes. Here, again, a financial advisor may be of help. Absent that, start by doing some research. Go to the library and enlist the librarian's help. Value Line has excellent information on individual stocks.

A diversified mutual fund may be a good choice if you are inexperienced at investing. Do some online research. Visit the websites of different mutual-fund companies and study the fact sheets on individual mutual funds.

> **Diversification** is the process of allocating your investment dollars to a broad number and range of securities in your portfolio that have different characteristics and perform differently from each other under different market conditions.

Call the mutual-fund company's 800 number (free service line) and speak to a representative about which funds are diversified.

Just as you had to learn new terminology when you bought a computer, you must also learn new terminology to invest effectively. I've said it once and I'll say it again: an excellent strategy is to subscribe to a financial newspaper or magazine, such as *The Wall Street Journal*. Another idea is to take out books on investing from the library. This is free research. It just costs you a little time, and as the old adage goes, "Invest your time before you invest your money."

The first thing to consider when investing in stocks is the size of the companies you want to invest in. *Large cap* is short for *large capitalization*. These are large companies. Capitalization means financial resources. So companies with large financial resources—lots of money—will be large companies. These companies tend to be less risky. *Mid-cap* means *mid-capitalization* or medium-sized companies. *Small-cap* is short for *small-capitalization*. These are small companies. Typically, small-cap companies have less financial resources, may be newer, and have fewer products to market. Small companies tend to be more volatile and more risky.

Growth companies are companies who are trying to achieve a high rate of growth in profits, size, and stock price. They plow all available money back into the company to fuel their growth. Therefore, they pay little or no dividend. Growth companies may be large, medium, or small in capitalization and size.

Value companies come in a few varieties. Usually you can buy them at a good value. One reason is that often they are recovering from a rough patch in their profitability, or a management shakeup. So you can pick them up inexpensively relative to their peers.

Some value companies are larger, more stable companies that prefer slow but steady growth. They may pay out good dividends to their shareholders rather than plowing their profits back into the company.

Growth and value tend to outperform counter-cyclically. That is, when one is up the other tends to be down and vice versa. That's why you need them both in your portfolio. The same might be said about large versus small companies, and domestic versus international companies. That's why you want a diversified portfolio.

ASSET ALLOCATION FUNDS

Asset allocation funds are typically "fund of funds"—that is, they have several different mutual funds inside of one overriding mutual fund. The underlying mutual funds each represent different segments of the market. Therefore, they have built in diversification. For that reason, asset allocation funds may be a good choice for the beginner investor, because they are already diversified. The important thing is to choose an asset allocation fund with the combination of stocks and bonds that matches your risk tolerance.

Because it is diversified, an asset-allocated portfolio may not outperform the latest "hot stock" or popular mutual fund. But, with the right asset allocation, you may be able to optimize the return on your entire portfolio with less risk. Some of the underlying funds will be outperforming, while some of the underlying funds will be underperforming. Overall, asset allocation portfolios tend to do well over time with less volatility.

ANNUITIES

There is one type of investment we have yet to cover, one that doesn't fall into the same category as stocks or bonds. This is called an *annuity*. I want to devote some time to annuities here because they can be excellent vehicles for producing retirement income.

An annuity is an insurance contract issued by an insurance company that guarantees certain promised benefits. These benefits are itemized in the contract and often provide some type of retirement income. Investments inside of the annuity grow tax-deferred until they are withdrawn. Withdrawals from an annuity prior to age 59½ will be subject to a 10 percent penalty, in addition to income taxes.

There are fixed annuities and variable annuities. Let's discuss fixed annuities first. There are two types of fixed annuities. The first type of fixed annuity guarantees the investor's principal, and offers a guaranteed interest rate for a specified period of time. The second type of fixed annuity has a market value adjustment (MVA) if the contract is surrendered prior to the rate guarantee period. This may result in a gain or loss of principal to the investor.[4]

Variable annuities are usually invested in mutual funds, which fluctuate with the market. Variable annuities are attractive in that they provide tax-deferred growth of the investments, plus income for retirement. Withdrawals from a non-qualified annuity (one that is not in a retirement account) do not have to be taken by age 70½ as is the case with retirement plans. Variable annuities

> One of the benefits of annuities is that they provide certain protections that help alleviate the downside effects of market fluctuations, such as guaranteed accumulation benefits or guaranteed income. Guaranteed accumulation benefits guarantee that your principal will grow by a certain percentage or to a specified dollar amount within a certain period of time, usually ten years. This benefit also protects your principal from going down with the market if it is left in the annuity for a stated period of time, again, usually ten years. Guaranteed accumulation benefit provides for a lump sum cash withdrawal at the end of the holding period that is equal to or greater than your original premium.
>
> *(Source: "Income Guarantees for Your Retirement Savings," Wells Fargo Advisors.)*

typically have living benefits, such as retirement income, which is of value to you during your lifetime.

Guaranteed withdrawal benefits guarantee the ability to withdraw a certain percentage of your initial investment (typically 4 percent to 7 percent) for a stated period of time, such as five, ten, fifteen, or twenty years or even over your lifetime. These benefits may have the potential to increase or "step up" as the market value increases.[5]

Guaranteed minimum income benefits provide a steady income stream for a specified number of years or for life, and may culminate in annuitization. These benefits create an income base that is based on your original principal plus a guaranteed growth rate over a specified number of years, usually ten. At the end of the growth years, income is paid out at a percentage (typically 4 percent to 7 percent) of the income base, or of the market value, if that is higher. This type of benefit provides consistent income.[6]

Annuities also offer *death benefits*, which provide a promised benefit to your beneficiaries when you die. Both living benefits and death benefits offer a menu of benefit options from which to choose. Each benefit has a cost, so typically you will choose those living benefits and death benefits that are appropriate for you.

Annuities can create a valuable, guaranteed stream of income for you during your retirement. Although they are not for everyone, they may be appropriate for part of your portfolio. Annuities require much understanding. Seek the help of a financial advisor who is knowledgeable in annuities. Consider doing a conference call with the financial advisor and the annuity company so that you can hear for yourself what all the benefits are, from which you may choose. Annuities are worth looking into, as they provide a variety of features, some of which may be of benefit to you or to your heirs.

THE POWER OF TAX-DEFERRED COMPOUNDING

One benefit of annuities is that the investments inside the annuity—typically mutual funds—grow tax-deferred. This means you don't pay taxes on the funds until you withdraw money from the annuity, usually in retirement. Over time, this can really add up.

The following table illustrates the power of tax deferral by examining the growth of two accounts—one taxable and one tax-deferred. Assuming a $25,000 initial investment and an annual return of 6 percent, the balance in the tax-deferred account, even after tax on withdrawals, is significantly higher than the taxable account, which has been taxed along the way.[7] Upon withdrawal, the funds in the annuity will be subject to the current ordinary income tax rate of the investor.

END OF YEAR	TAX-DEFERRED ACCOUNT	TAXABLE ACCOUNT	$ DIFFERENCE
Compounding at 6%, 25% Tax Bracket after tax			
1	$26,125	$26,125	$0
5	$31,342	$31,155	$187
10	$39,828	$38,824	$1,004
20	$66,384	$60,293	$6,091
30	$113,940	$93,633	$20,308

*This illustration is provided for informational purposes only and is not intended to represent an actual investment.

INFLATION—OR WHEN DID EVERYTHING GET TO BE SO EXPENSIVE?

Inflation simply means *rising prices*. We have all experienced the rising cost of oil, gasoline, milk, food, tuition, and health care. We understand inflation in the present tense. But surprisingly few people understand inflation in the future tense.

From 1922 to 2004, inflation has averaged about 3.04 percent annually. That means that prices of everyday consumer goods, such as food, gas, and housing, have risen on average 3.04 percent every year. According to the St. Louis Federal Reserve Board, the Consumer Price Index, which is a measure of inflation, increased at a 2.9 percent compounded annual rate of change from 1985 to 2010, or 102.7 percent total. That doesn't seem like much. But look out. For in those twenty-five years—which might have been someone's retirement—consumer prices more than doubled.

Let's say you retire at age sixty-five with $400,000 in savings. In twenty years, if inflation has averaged 3 percent to 4 percent per year, you will only be able to buy $200,000 worth of food, rent, health care, and necessities.[8] Inflation can devastate even the most carefully drawn financial plan. It dilutes the value of our money, so we can't buy as much of the things we need.

We underestimate the effect of inflation on our future. Inflation is insidious. When we first retire, prices are what they are, and subconsciously we just expect them to remain the same. As we move into the middle retirement years, we begin to feel the effects of inflation on our budget. Everything costs more. We know it is happening, because we see the prices of things, but no one ever put a line item for inflation on their retirement budget. We need to save more than we think we will need.

According to the Bureau of Labor Statistics, you would need to have almost three times as much saved in today's dollars—$274,550—to buy the same amount of consumer goods, such as food, gas, clothing, and shelter, etc., as just $100,000 would have bought approximately thirty years earlier in 1980. See for yourself at (http://www.bls.gov/data/inflation_calculator.htm). Many people spend thirty years in retirement, especially if they retire early. This is why inflation is so detrimental to retirement savings.

THE EFFECT OF INFLATION ON YOUR INVESTMENTS

Inflation also affects your investments. Here's how. Let's say you earn 8 percent return on your investments, and inflation is at 3 percent. Your *real rate of return*, after inflation is figured in, is only 5 percent. That is because we subtract inflation from your return.

8% investment return - 3% inflation = 5% real rate of return

The **real rate of return** is the return you receive on your investments after the effects of inflation are factored in.

To summarize, a 3 percent inflation rate will cause consumer prices to double over the course of twenty-four years. Armed with this knowledge, we could reasonably expect that over the course of our own twenty-four-plus-year retirement, consumer prices will double if inflation averages 3 percent. So how can we protect ourselves from this?

The hard truth may be that we either increase our savings by 1½ to 2 times, or expect to cut our standard of living in half by the end of our retirement years. Doubling our savings is a tall order. So here are some other solutions.

HOW TO PROTECT YOUR RETIREMENT FROM INFLATION

1. *Invest in stocks.* Stocks are generally considered to have some protection against inflation over time. The reason is simple. When you own a stock, you own that corporation. Corporations usually produce a product or a service. If their cost to produce that product or service increases, they will try to pass on that cost increase to the buyers of their products or services. That helps to maintain the value of the corporation, and therefore your stock. Furthermore, if you invest in stocks that also pay dividends, you will have a source of income. And, good companies tend to raise their dividends—many do so yearly—and that, too, will help hedge against inflation.

2. *Annuities*. Some annuities offer benefits that may protect against inflation. Annuities can be complex and may require the assistance of a financial advisor to help interpret and understand the benefits. Take some time to research the various annuity products to match the right one to your needs.

3. *Other inflation-resistant investments*. Some investments, known as "hard assets," such as gold or real estate, have historically been considered to act as a hedge against inflation. This is not guaranteed, as both are cyclical (go up and down in value) and tend to be subject to the law of supply and demand. Gold trades on "sentiment," or how the public feels about the economy. Gold pays no dividends, so it does not create a stream of income for retirement. Real estate values depend on location and incomes, so real estate may or may not keep up with inflation. With real estate there is a huge carrying cost—the mortgage. That said, if the mortgage is reasonable and can be paid off by retirement age, a home might be a better safety net and hedge against inflation than renting.

4. *The Retirement What-If Game.* If you are thinking about retiring, play this game with yourself: Pretend all of your expenses are double what they currently are. Could you still retire? If not, consider the next strategy.

5. *Wait to retire.* An effective strategy against inflation is to wait to retire. Keep working longer than you think you need to.

6. *Delay taking Social Security.* Unless you are in ill health or in dire need of money, delay taking Social Security for as long as possible. For many of us, Social Security is the only "pension" we will receive. By waiting to take Social Security, we can greatly increase this pension income stream for life. In fact, every year we wait, our Social Security benefit increases by 8 percent. The difference between what we would receive if we took Social Security as soon as we are eligible (currently sixty-two) and what we would receive if we waited until the maximum age (currently seventy) is a whopping 76 percent! (Source: Social Security.) It might be better to consider spending down other assets earlier in retirement to forestall taking Social Security to secure a larger benefit.

7. *Cut costs via downsizing or non-traditional living arrangements.* One way to foil the effects of inflation is by cutting costs, and one of the most effective ways to do this is through downsizing or non-traditional living arrangements. For women who may have experienced widowhood or divorce, often their primary investment is their home. As I've said in earlier chapters, consider getting a roommate or renting out unused rooms, or if necessary, downsizing your home.

8. *Always Be Earning (ABE).* Maintain an earnings income stream throughout your retirement. Buy investments that will pay you back forever, such as dividend-paying stocks, certain annuities, and income-producing mutual funds. Keep your day job. Don't retire just because you reach a specific age. Retire when you and your financial advisor determine that it would be highly unlikely for you to run out of money. In this era of corporate cost-cutting and downsizing, it may be difficult for near-retirees and retirement-age adults to keep their jobs. If you get downsized, immediately seek another full-time job, even if they offer you a retirement buy-out—which may or may

not be enough for your full retirement—and even if you have to accept a lesser salary. If you can't find full-time employment, get a part-time job (or two).

9. *Create income from your own business.* If they won't hire you, hire yourself. But remember that this is not a hobby. It is a positive and creative survival strategy that needs to produce income from the start.

10. *Create several stackable income streams.* Some income streams are more resistant to inflation, such as a pension with a cost of living adjustment (COLA), and some income streams may simply not last throughout the years of your retirement, such as alimony. The more reliable income streams you can stack, the better.

11. *Consult with a financial advisor* who understands the effects of inflation and can do some intermediate and long-term projections on your financial plan.

12. *Have a plan.* Just having a retirement plan and updating it regularly greatly increases the odds of your success in retirement.

REFERENCES:

1 Brinson, Singer and Beebower, "Determinants of Portfolio Performance," Financial Analysts Journal, May/June 1991, as quoted in "From Here to There: A Clear View of Retirement for Women," Wells Fargo Advisors.

2 Stewart, James B. "The Asset-Allocation Fallacy." *The Wall St. Journal*, April 9-10, 2011.

3 Mincer, Jilian. "Hidden Risks in Target Funds." April 9-10, 2011.

4 "Annuities – An Important Part of Your Retirement Portfolio," Wells Fargo Advisors.

5 Source: "Income Guarantees for Your Retirement Savings," Wells Fargo Advisors.

6 Ibid.

7 "Annuities – An Important Part of Your Retirement Portfolio," Wells Fargo Advisors.

8 *Ernst & Young's Retirement Planning Guide*. John Wiley & Sons, 2002, p. 29 (see chart).

Chapter 10

Step Six:
Building a Profitable Business

A hundred years ago, women took to the workforce in whatever capacity they were allowed—as seamstresses, cooks, or shopkeepers. Today women seem more reluctant than ever to start their own businesses. And yet, doing so may be one of the best ways to provide a potentially unlimited stream of income.

If you have a talent or hobby, consider developing it into a home-based business. Chances are you already have the skill set and tools to get started without a major investment. Small businesses have many advantages: access to increased income, business tax write-offs, and group benefits coverage.

The Internet has made starting a home-based business so much easier. You could set up a virtual storefront and choose your own hours. Enjoy the freedom to market whatever product or service will make you happy. Then make it lucrative. Plan, enjoy, and prosper.

Another option is to invest in a turnkey business. In other words: buy a franchise. Just be careful to do your homework on the franchisor before investing any money. Talk to an attorney who specializes in franchises, as well as other franchisees, to ensure that you protect yourself legally. Buying a franchise generally means cutting through a lot of red tape, and having an expert by your side is a crucial element to your success. Learn about franchises on the SBA website: www.sba.gov/community/blogs/buying-franchise.com.

In this chapter, we'll look at several ways to start a business. We will also see how the Strong sisters took this lesson to heart, blazing new terrain as entrepreneurs and impacting not only their lives but also the lives of those around them.

STEP ONE
GENERATE AND RESEARCH YOUR IDEA

Many women have a hobby that could become a cash cow—something they love doing but have never dreamed of monetizing. Don't underestimate the value of your painting, knitting, sewing, handicraft, writing, speaking, music, and various other skills. Do you know how to cook? Start a catering company. Can you sew?

Put those skills to use making children's clothing or designer gowns. Do you have a memoir in you? Write it!

To monetize: to convert an asset into or establish something as money or legal tender.

(Source: www.investopedia.com)

Let us return to Sara, the youngest Strong sister, who in Chapter 4 had just begun to take her passion for knitting to the next level. After doing her prep work—researching market trends and determining the best ways to sell her work online—she launches her business, "Unique Knit." The websites that bring her the most business are Etsy and Handmade Catalog, so she focuses the bulk of her marketing energies there. She begins advertising unique sweaters, scarves, and hats that are fun and festive.

Before long, she is receiving orders. At first there aren't many, but that's okay: this gives Sara time to focus on fulfilling each order above and beyond the customer's expectations. She makes this her personal mission and it really shows. Her customers are thrilled with the products as well as the service they receive. Sara's next step is to handpick a dozen happy customers, and she asks them if they would be willing to write her an online review. Their answer is unanimously, "Yes!"

Suddenly, Sara is getting five-star reviews and referrals begin rolling in. She extends her nightly knitting schedule so that she has more time to fill orders. With the holiday season looming, people are eager to buy unique knit pieces to give as gifts, and Sara realizes that soon she may need to hire a fellow knitter to meet demand!

Inspired by her little sister's success, Debbie begins to reconsider her own feelings about starting an online business. What if there was a way she, too, could monetize her artistic talents? Growing up, she was always the "artistic one"—as a child it was Debbie who corralled her sisters into doing arts and crafts projects, and in college she worked as a studio art assistant painting huge murals around campus. Of course, as the sole proprietor of her freelance contracting business, she put her own art to the wayside years ago, focusing instead on keeping her business alive.

As she watches Sara grow her business, Debbie realizes it may be time to dust off her artistic skills and see if she can put them to use. She had already begun the research for a small business loan; is this the right time to revisit that idea? Though she once balked at the notion of starting a business on the Internet, she realizes this is where the future is going. The more candidly she looks at her finances, the more she realizes her savings are seriously depleted. Starting a sideline business is not actually a wild idea; it is a judicious one.

After a frank discussion with her sisters, Debbie decides to take action. She enrolls in an online course from the Small Business Administration at www.SBA. gov to learn some basic tools for making money on the Internet, all the while actively brainstorming what product she wants to bring to the marketplace. She's realistic enough to know it needs to be something that won't be physically taxing or demanding—because of her health issues, she is long past the point of staying up until 2 a.m. painting murals like she did in her college days.

Then genius strikes. Debbie has always loved clever T-shirts, and she sees them more and more, especially since she lives in a college town filled with young people and hip dressers. The funny thing is, anytime Debbie sees a slogan on a T-shirt, she can usually come up with three off the top of her head that are even more catchy and clever—and she can visualize a sharp, eye-catching design to match.

The more she thinks about her idea, the more excited she becomes. She starts to dream about starting a T-shirt company called, "Tees, please!" She will combine her unique and beautiful artwork with wise historical (and therefore out of copyright) sayings from genius minds, such as Shakespeare, Goethe, and Emerson. For example, on the front of a T-shirt, she will use Shakespeare's line from Hamlet, "To thine own self be true." And on the back of the T-shirt, she will have the line "I'm true to Nantucket."

She will artistically silk screen beautiful images from Nantucket on the front and back of the T-shirt. Debbie figures she can use this same motif with any number of tourist locations. She also believes she can use this same concept with colleges—starting with the one in her own town. The slogan for the college tees will read "I'm true to Ivylove College," incorporating her artwork of the most famous landmark from Ivylove College, its historic clock tower. Again, it's a business concept that can be applied to colleges and universities everywhere.

However, since Debbie has been actively strengthening her financial literacy, she knows there is significant work to be done before blazing boldly ahead. She decides her next step is to draft a business plan.

STEP TWO
DRAFT A BUSINESS PLAN

Many aspiring entrepreneurs do not appreciate just how valuable a written business plan can be. A business plan acts as a roadmap to guide you. It serves as a benchmark to measure your progress. It is also required for financing—if you are applying for a loan, the loan officer is going to need to see where you plan to take your business and exactly how it will be profitable.

Before you begin drafting your business plan, define your mission statement. The mission statement defines *who* you are and *what* you do. Be concise. For example, Debbie Strong's mission statement is this: "It is my mission to be the most sought-after online retailer of fun, clever T-shirts in the tri-city region."

Next is strategy. Strategy tells *how* you will achieve your mission statement. How will you make your business successful? How will you differentiate yourself and add value? Some of Debbie's ideas include specifics about her T-shirt designs—what makes them clever *and* classy, drawing on the sayings of great artists and thinkers as opposed to some of the more crude tees she's seen. She will set herself apart by making funny T-shirts that are also beautiful to look at, and she is already in touch with several graphic design teams she has worked with in the past who can make that dream a reality.

Next you'll want to perform a SWOT analysis. A SWOT analysis identifies your *strengths* and *weaknesses*, and the *opportunities* and *threats* in the marketplace. Emphasize your strengths. Outsource your weaknesses (for example, payroll). Take advantage of the opportunities in the marketplace, such as the Internet. Know what might threaten your business, such as competition from cheap labor overseas.

This is a very real threat for Debbie: early in her

research she discovers there are literally hundreds of T-shirt companies that ship products from Bangalore and Taiwan, which could seriously undercut her market share. But then Debbie decides to turn her biggest threat into her biggest strength: She finds a way to outsource the actual manufacturing of the shirts, working with a company that gives her amazing rates. This will then allow her to price her products competitively.

The next step is to create a marketing strategy around the 5 Ps: people, product, place, price, and promotion.

- *People:* Whom will you sell to? Target your market. Whom will you hire?
- *Product:* What type of product or service will you offer? Define your niche.
- *Place:* Where will you locate your business? What type of distribution channel will you have?
- *Price:* How much will you charge? How does that compare with your competitors?
- *Promotion:* How will you get the word out? How will you create a cohesive advertising strategy? Define your target audience, media, and budget. For example, Debbie is already preparing email blasts and a vibrant Facebook marketing campaign.

Your financial projections will be a critical component of your business plan—more on that momentarily. Where do you want to be in one, three, and five years? What do you expect your revenues and expenses will be? Create strong, professional financial statements. Show positive trends.

And finally, have an exit strategy. Incorporate a retirement plan into your business model from the start. Think about business succession planning long before you'll need it. Perhaps the most lucrative thing you can do is to start your business with the intent to sell it for a handsome profit.

"Women entrepreneurs need to learn that they can and should play in the Olympics of business: starting, building, and selling a company successfully," says author Ann M. Holmes, who describes selling her business for "millions" in her book *There's a Business in Every Woman*. Ann goes on to say this: "For the owner of a privately held company, getting out is the end point of the game. The company you start is an investment; after a marriage and children, it is likely the largest presence in your life, consuming substantial time, money and emotional resources. As with any other investment, the goal is to get the best possible return. In the case of a company, the returns come mainly when you sell it."

(Source: Holmes, Ann M. There's a Business in Every Woman, Ballantine Books: 2008, p. 27-28)

If you are thinking about starting a business, I encourage you to start small. I have seen many women who go out and create a business without the income to support it—and I have been guilty of doing the same thing myself. You set up the office and the phone and the website. You order the dazzling new stationery and business cards—all the accoutrements—but you don't have the income yet. This is a surefire recipe for disaster.

I strongly believe that if you are a new small business owner, you should only take out a loan to finance the production of your "widgets" when you have a purchase order in hand. Too many small businesses start with a loan before they have the cash flow confidently in place. Then they have a loan (debt) without income (cash flow). Start small. Build your business one step at a time and wait to borrow until your business is more mature and has solid trends in sales and cash flows.

It is far better to start with one widget in humble surroundings, sell it, and make two more. Once you sell two, make three. Sell three and make six. Sell six and make eight. You do not want to build a business for the sake of building a business; you want it to be profitable. You want an income-producing business. From day one, you really want to see the income. This is why income statements are key to your success.

If you are thinking about starting a business, have done *extensive* market research, and gained experience in that particular industry, you may feel the time is right to apply for financing for your business. You can obtain a small business loan through a variety of channels. These include a traditional bank loan, a loan from the Small Business Administration or other government agency, interested investors, such as friends or family, and "angel" investors or venture capital investors. Many women end up funding their business by raiding their own savings or retirement funds. *I am strongly opposed to using the very savings for retirement that we are trying to build up—not deplete.* Later, we will discuss other ways to fund your business.

HOW TO WRITE A FORMAL BUSINESS PLAN FOR FINANCING

You will need a formal business plan and financial statements to obtain financing for your business. The Small Business Administration (SBA) has an excellent website to help you formulate and write a business plan. (www.sba.gov/business-plan). It also has a nifty interactive tool to help you write your business plan step by step. Debbie went on the SBA.gov website and used the interactive tool. This helped her think about her "Tees, please!" business with greater depth and clarity.

The Small Business Administration also oversees Women's Business Centers (WBCs) with 110 offices nationwide. The WBCs provide a variety of services to help women business owners succeed, such as training, counseling, seminars on financial topics, and help with the SBA loan application process.

A good business plan has a formal structure that incorporates specific elements. An excellent resource for small businesses is *The Small Business Bible* by Steven D. Strauss, which contains a wealth of information for small businesses, plus an outstanding example of a professional business plan.

The basic elements of a formal business plan include the following:

Title Page

The title page contains the name of the company, the logo and website, if you have one, as well as the name, address, phone, and email of the business owner.

Executive Summary

The executive summary is your opportunity to enthusiastically engage the investor in the excitement of your company. In three to four pages, it summarizes your company, your vision for your company, your company's product and marketing plans, and of course, growth and financial projections. It conveys what is unique about your product or service and tells why this is the right time and the right market for your company. It discusses the market for your product, whom you will sell to, and your strategy for manufacturing, marketing, pricing, promoting, and delivering your product or service.

It should also include information on when your company was formed, its legal structure, where it is located, and who the key officers are. Briefly delineate the amount of financing you are seeking.

Many sources suggest writing the executive summary last, after you have thoroughly thought through all the components of your business. Another approach is to write it once in bullet points to get you started, and then rewrite it when you are finished with the business plan.

The executive summary is your best opportunity to captivate the interest and imagination of the lender about the excitement of your business. If you fail to ignite interest in the Executive Summary, the lender may not read much further, so be thorough, concise, interesting, and build in the "wow factor."

Table of Contents

The table of contents lists the various section titles of the business plan with page numbers, for ease of reading.

Business Description

In this section you will need to describe your business and its legal structure. You will also define your company's unique product or service, the market for your product or service, and what need your product will satisfy. You should define how your business will position itself—for example, wholesaler, retailer, manufacturer, etc.—and include operational plans for producing and delivering your product.

Market Analysis

Here you will summarize your market research on your business's particular industry. After you describe the specific need your product will meet, you need to define the market for your product. How large is the market for your product? Quantify it in numbers. Specifically identify your niche market, as you cannot be all things to all people. Is the market local and small, national, e-commerce via the Internet, or international? What part or share of the market (give a percentage estimate, if possible) do you expect you will capture? Is the market for your product expected to keep growing? How strong is the demand for your product or service expected to be? What factors might alter that demand?

Management

You will need to convey strength and confidence in your management team to convince financiers to lend you money. List the credentials and experience of the management team. If you are a sole proprietor or start-up, you may need to draw strength from your council of advisors. Consult with each of them and ask their permission to list them as a member of your team. Highlight their credentials and experience. Do they have any other recommendations for your team? Enlist their help in further building your team and your business.

Your team should include an attorney, CPA, head of marketing, chief operations officer, sales manager, financial advisor, insurer, and any other appropriate consultants, whose credentials and experience you can call upon and utilize.

Product or Service

What is your company's product or service? Describe the features and benefits that make it outstanding. What is exciting, different, better about your product? In what stage of its lifecycle is the product or service—is it still on the drawing board, do you have a prototype, or do you have an extensive inventory with a history of fast turnover of sales, in which case you would give sales statistics? Do you have intellectual property, such as design copyrights or patents? Will you need research and development dollars? If so, define how much time and money you will need.

How will you price your product? How and where will you produce your product? What logistics do you need to have in place to deliver your products—a website? Delivery trucks?

What makes your product so unique that the end consumer *must* have it? This is known as your unique selling proposition. It's what sets you apart. Emphasize your difference in the marketplace.

Competitive Analysis

Who are your competitors? How big are they and how long have they been in business? Where are they located? What advantages do they have over you—size? financial resources? What do they do well? What do they *not* do well?

How will you compete with them—on price? Can you provide greater convenience or speed of delivery? Unique concept or design? What factor gives you an edge over them? Be as specific as you can about your competition and use actual data if possible, such as annual sales, sales per square foot, growth trends, profitability, etc.

Marketing

Marketing is your strategy for obtaining customers and growing your business. Strategy means "how." How will you get your first customer—cold-calling or networking? Can you legally and ethically take loyal customers with you from your current company?

Who are your ideal clients? How will you reach them? Will you hire sales people, or will you use independent sales representatives? What is your big idea for selling your big idea (product or service)? How will you produce it, price it, deliver it? What is your distribution channel?

Marketing also includes advertising, publicity, and promotion. How often will you communicate with your customers? What message will you give them to stimulate them to buy your product? Will you use advertising—through the Internet, traditional channels, or both? Will you use promotions, such as sales, and if so, how often? Will you pair up with charities to hold events that will create a buzz and give you some invaluable free publicity?

How will you grow your company? Again, identify your ideal customer and the best way to reach and serve them. Then turn them into repeat customers, so that they buy again and again, even if it is only an accessory or part. For example, if you sell a coffee maker, sell them the coffee, too. Better still, can you structure your sales so that they are continual, such as on retainer or by monthly subscription?

Another growth strategy is to duplicate your best customers. Cloning your customers is one of the best ways to grow your business. Reward them with incentives to refer their friends, family, and colleagues. Another excellent growth strategy is to duplicate your business model, perhaps in another location. Just look at the successful growth Starbucks has had by cloning its business model in different locations worldwide.

Review your marketing plan regularly. Always be on the lookout for new marketing ideas. Exchange ideas with others in your field at trade shows or association meetings. Stay fresh.

Sales

Your business cannot succeed without sales. If you are just starting out and don't have sales yet, you will have to make an educated estimate as to how much you believe you can actually sell annually, monthly, quarterly. If you don't know, don't just hazard a guess. Do market research. What are your competitors' sales? Consult with knowledgeable people, such as your accountant, your trade association president, or even friendly competitors, to see what your expectations should be for first and subsequent year sales and growth rates. Will you grow by 10 percent per year? 20 percent? 30 percent?

What are your assumptions based on? Define your assumptions and the reasons you believe they are sound.

Who will sell your product or service—you? If not you, will you hire someone? How will you find the right person or team? What is their sales track record? What standards will you set for your sales force? How will you measure the level of their activities and success? In revenue, units sold, new customers?

Financial Analysis, Projections, and Funding Request

Financial analysis is a critical component of the business plan. Lenders look very closely at your financial statements, assumptions, projections and trends (if you have a business history). Financial statements are like vital signs—they tell the health of your business at a glance. If you have three to five years' historical financial statements with positive trends, you are in a great position. You probably also have a good understanding of what is required to fund and financially manage a business. Work with your financial officer or accountant to make sure these are in good order, and show your business in the best light.

If you do not have three to five years' worth of financial statements, you will have to be creative, strong, and perseverant—and should probably keep your day job for now. Without raiding your retirement savings, can you fund and manage your business for three years, possibly with the help of family or simply by starting small and building? Even if you are small, you can create positive growth rates and profit trends, and clean, organized financial statements that will impress a lender. During those three years, you can acquire the knowledge, management skill and experience to then be able to manage formal funding.

. . . .

Financial analysis is the reason that I became a financial advisor. I was a small business owner, designing and manufacturing jewelry that I sold to Tiffany & Co., among others. I designed, sourced materials, manufactured, and sold my jewelry every waking hour that I wasn't working at my day job. I started my day at 4:30 a.m. to make sure that I delivered my orders on time.

Every day on my lunch hours, I called retail buyers to set up appointments to show them my jewelry. My day job enabled me to work weekends so that I could have days off during the week to make sales calls, buy supplies, and deliver my goods. I was very knowledgeable about jewelry and gems, but I didn't know anything about finance. I knew that finance was my Achilles heel and could take my business down entirely if I made a financial misstep.

The first time I applied for a loan, I went to the big bank, a total novice. I took a purchase order from Tiffany to show them that I had a means to pay back the loan. I needed funding to finance the gold, silver, and gemstones that I would need to complete the order for Tiffany. The banker gave me the loan, but he stated on the loan application that the purpose was to buy furniture. I could not understand why the purchase of household furniture was a better investment than a purchase order from the venerated and financially sound Tiffany & Co.!

That was my moment of enlightenment. That was the moment I knew I needed to acquire a strong foundation of financial knowledge. I decided to go back to school for an MBA in finance. It wasn't easy. I had to take entrance exams and math refresher courses. The dean of the business school didn't understand why I insisted on a concentration in finance. With my design background, marketing would be much easier. They were right. Finance was not the easiest course for someone who had spent fifteen years as a designer. But finance was the education I came to get. While I was getting my MBA, I decided to take a job on Wall Street to learn its ways from the inside. Unfamiliar as it was, this, too, was a challenge and an eye opener.

As a financial professional, I was shocked by the disparity in income and retirement benefits between men and women. I needn't have been. It's all right there in the census data. In 1967, women earned about 58 cents to a man's dollar.[1] It *has* gotten better—now women earn roughly 77 cents to a man's dollar, so the income gap is narrowing. Still, over the course of their working lives, that income gap is estimated to have cost women over $400,000—and in some cases, well over $700,000.[2] I've said it before, but I am struck by the idea that that half-million-dollar-plus cumulative income gap would have served women well as a nice retirement nest egg.

My financial education has proven its usefulness many times over. It is one reason why I have such a passion to help women plan for retirement. I know what *I* didn't know about finance. I understand what women in general don't know about finance. And I now know how to help women achieve financial security. The answer is to create SISTERS—several Stackable Income Streams To Empower Retirement Security. And for this, you need some understanding of finance.

. . . .

You will need three to five years of historical financial statements and three to five years of financial projections to apply for a loan. Take your time with this. Work closely with your accountant. Be a sleuth. Gather as much financial information about your industry and competitors as you can to provide realistic projections for your business. Always define the assumptions you are making about your financial projections and provide a strong basis or reference for your argument. For example, how much do you expect to grow your business every year (this is your growth rate)—10 percent? 25 percent?—and what is that assumption based on? How does that compare to your industry average?

"The key to understanding your company's financial situation is maintaining up-to-date records detailing every cent going into and coming out of your business. Managing cash flow is the key to keeping your business open."

(Source: Holmes, Ann M. There's a Business in Every Woman, Ballantine Books: 2008, p. 83-84)

Debbie Strong is very excited about her T-shirt business. She enjoys the creative challenge of the Small Business Administration's interactive tool to help her write her business plan. Debbie has thought through a thorough manufacturing, marketing, sales, and distribution plan.

However, when it comes to the financials, Debbie is stumped. She consults Marilyn, who has promised to help her with the books. Marilyn knows they need to bring in more knowledgeable financial professionals to help them with their business plan and funding request. They meet with their financial advisor, accountant, and counselors at the Small Business Administration.

After much soul searching, Debbie decides that requesting a loan might be premature, based on her experience and lack of history. Debbie decides to take advantage of the SBA online course in finance, business, management, and writing a business plan, while gradually starting the business on her own.

Recognizing that she will need financial resources, Debbie approaches Wanda about non-traditional residence sharing. Since her husband died several years ago, and the kids went off to college, Wanda has extra bedrooms and bathrooms, and her late husband's unused tool shop in the basement. Debbie negotiates with Wanda to move into one of the bedrooms and move her art studio into the tool shop in the basement. That way, Debbie will cut her rent in half—thereby giving her funds to support her T-shirt start-up business—and Wanda will have income from the unused space in her home. That benefits everyone!

STEP THREE
START A SISTERS CLUB

If there is one message you take away from this book, I hope it is that saving for retirement alongside other women is infinitely preferable to doing it alone. This is certainly true for starting a business. It does not take Debbie long to realize she needs to create a supportive community to help get her fledgling T-shirt business off the ground.

Lucky for Debbie, her sister Sara is the perfect partner for such a union, since Sara has just recently launched Unique Knit. The two sisters begin meeting once a week, and before long, they realize they want to extend their network even farther. They decide it is time to start a SISTERS Club.

SISTERS Clubs are similar to book clubs in that you get together regularly to discuss exciting topics. Only in this case, the exciting topic is sharing ideas of how to start businesses and create more stackable income streams for retirement. Starting a business with other women opens you up to many additional opportunities, such as the possibility of tax advantages and group benefits coverage. And, increased income opportunities give you extra cash to travel and have more fun.

Excited by the idea of creating their own SISTERS Club, Debbie and Sara carefully select a group of talented women and invite them to join forces and share their skill sets. They look for partners and teammates with talents they need but may not have. Debbie teams up with women who have more financial savvy, and Sara seeks out peers with more managerial experience, as well as fellow knitters. Together, these women pool their resources to create an environment of emotional and social support.

You, too, can create a SISTERS Club. If you are a fantastic artist, find two other women who are great at bookkeeping and marketing, respectively. If you are a dynamite bookkeeper or marketer, look for women brimming with great ideas for a new product or service that will take the world by storm. Get creative. The goal is to start a SISTERS Club in which you create a circle of friends all striving to create Stackable Income Streams To Empower Retirement Security in their own lives.

I believe that every woman should consider creating collaborative economic teams for financial success. This is paramount. Women must create and fund their own retirement plans to generate money in retirement. No one else will do it for you. But that doesn't mean you have to do it all alone.

What kind of businesses could women start if we pooled our resources and put our heads together? The sky is truly the limit. How about a cosmetics company? It worked for Mary Kay Ash. Or how about a home and lifestyle media company? It worked for Martha Stewart. How about starting a television media company? Oprah accomplished that and then some. Does it all sound too complicated? Just start a cookie company, then. Mrs. Fields did. So did the Girl Scouts!

A word to the wise: *Be sure to keep your day job to pay your bills and maintain your benefits while you build your business.* The excitement of starting a new business can be invigorating and empowering; for many women it fast becomes the most thrilling thing in their lives. But I strongly suggest that you keep your day job, at least in the early stages of growing your business. This will ensure that you have the medical benefits and income to continue building your retirement dreams.

STEP FOUR
DEVELOP A COUNCIL OF ADVISORS

Once you have formed a SISTERS Club, develop a council of professional advisors, such as CPAs, attorneys, financial advisors, insurance specialists, lenders, and estate planners. Competent advisors can guide you on your road to success.

Sara and Debbie take a very tactical approach to building their SISTERS Club. They scout out a financial advisor, a CPA, a bookkeeper, a banker, an insurance specialist, and two attorneys, one of whom specializes in small Internet companies. The idea is to have a network of strong, capable women they can call on for advice.

SISTERS Clubs are particularly attractive for women who have been forced out of the workforce through downsizing or who are having difficulty finding employment. If they won't hire you, hire yourself. You're too young to give up.

There is just one caveat—and this is important. SISTERS Clubs must be *profitable from the start*. That means your business must *earn* income from the get-go, not simply spend money, time, and resources creating a business. So how can your SISTERS Club be profitable from the start? By starting small and continuously consulting with your council of advisors. They will help keep you on track.

STEP FIVE
ESTABLISH CONTRACTS

It takes Debbie and Sara a few months to populate their SISTERS Club—a few women come to one meeting but have to drop out for personal reasons. However, after a short while, a "core group" emerges. There are six women who are serious about pursuing their dreams and doing so within a larger community of friends and colleagues.

Now is the time to establish "contractual arrangements of fairness." Think of it like a prenup. SISTERS Clubs who want to collaborate in any kind of business venture need to establish contractual arrangements of fairness. By spelling out everything in advance—such as roles and responsibilities—it solidifies the way the group functions, as well as helps avoid arguments later.

Lucky for the Strong sisters, the other attorney in the group specializes in contracts. She helps draw up a contractual agreement that everyone can be happy with. Then the women sit around a table together, iron out the remaining issues, and move forward into a collaboration that will mutually benefit everyone involved.

STEP SIX
CREATE A GLOBAL COMMUNITY

Within six months, Debbie and Sara have created a thriving group of women who are helping each other in a myriad of ways. After an intensive round of schedule juggling, they settle on meeting twice monthly at a downtown restaurant they all adore. The women freely call on each other throughout the week, too, asking for advice or assistance. Every one of them feels both supported by the others and useful to their colleagues. The Strong sisters are proud of establishing such a spirited community with a healthy practice of give-and-take.

They are having so much fun; even Wanda is considering joining the Club! She has been looking at investing in a franchise of a local sandwich shop, but before she moves forward, Debbie and Sara invite her to come sit in on several SISTERS meetings as a kind of preemptive tack. This will give her the flavor of what it is like to launch a business while also encouraging her to pause and consider what needs to be done first.

A year passes, then two, and the women's businesses begin to thrive. They experience spikes in profit, and the ways they help one another continue to evolve. As their profits grow, they work with the financial advisor on their Council of Advisors to develop an investment portfolio. She shows them how to buy high-quality dividend stocks. When the dividends get paid out, she suggests that they reinvest them to keep growing their stock positions. That's one way "money goes to money." Additionally, she recommends they also invest in a diversified mutual fund of high-quality, short-term bonds to balance the dividend stocks.

Wanda ultimately decides to invest in the franchise and spends many months laying the groundwork for her eventual ROI (return on investment). Sara's knitting business expands enough that she hires three additional knitters, as well as opens up a physical shop in a cute storefront downtown. Debbie is the beneficiary of some lucky publicity—a local TV news program interviews her about her T-shirt company, and suddenly she experiences a healthy boost in sales.

But the Strong sisters don't stop there. Because of all the success and happiness they are enjoying in their own lives, they decide to take their SISTERS Club to the next level. They propose to the other women that they expand their economic base through a worldwide network of SISTERS Clubs—a virtual community. They could support each other financially by buying each other's products, not to mention offer emotional and social support.

The other women love the idea. They are all eager to share the joy and added financial security they have experienced from the club. Why not spread the wealth?

One of the women is a social media guru, so she charts out a way for their SISTERS Club to communicate and interact with other SISTERS Clubs through Internet websites, blogs, emails, friendly competitions, rallies, and other SISTERS events.

Does this sound far-fetched? It shouldn't. If you have ever been to a Harley-Davidson event, you know the kind of global community I am talking about. Harley owners gather to ride, party, raise funds for charity, meet their brethren, and show off their beautiful bikes (and buy a few more accessories). It's a "hog" community!

WHY NOT?

If starting a business is not for you, that is perfectly fine. There are many other ways to create stackable income streams, as we have seen in this book. But if any of this has struck a chord with you—if you have found yourself reading this chapter and feeling a flicker of excitement, thinking to yourself, "Yes! I could do that!"—then I suggest you explore the idea in greater depth. Why not?

Cash flow is fun. Building a business is fun. Creating and growing a profitable investment portfolio is fun. Disposable income is fun. Creating and living a *carefree* retirement life is fun. No worries. When was the last time you could stop worrying, and breathe? Or laugh?

Take the Strong sisters as an example again. Marilyn is the one sister who has been sitting on the sidelines as her sisters create their own businesses. She sees how this new burst of energy is impacting her sisters' lives for the better, and while she is not interested in starting a business herself, she decides she wants to find a way to participate.

She doesn't have Sara's great fashion sense or the knitting abilities to start a clothing line. And with her husband and kids, she doesn't really have the time to pursue buying a franchise like Wanda or selling T-shirts online like Debbie. But what she *does* have is accounting prowess, since she has been keeping her family's accounts in order for years.

So Marilyn offers to do payroll and accounting for her sisters' businesses. They are all delighted by the idea. Marilyn's financial knowledge makes their businesses run more smoothly, while also giving her the great satisfaction of using her time-honed skills to help grow her sisters' businesses. It also earns Marilyn a seat at the SISTERS Club, where she loves interacting with other smart, savvy women—reminding her that she and her sisters aren't the only ones who are "Strong"!

I encourage you to get creative and think outside the box as you consider starting your own business. The more non-traditional strategies you consider, the more exciting the future becomes. Here is a recap of some steps you might take:

- Start profitable home-based businesses using the skills, talent, and tools you already own.
- Create collaborative economic teams to devise ways to create lifetime income for retirement: SISTERS Clubs.
- Pool your resources, talent, and skills.
- Develop a council of specialized advisors.
- Have in place contractual arrangements of fairness to avoid conflicts.
- Tap into a community of SISTERS Clubs around the world for dynamic idea-sharing, moral support, and marketing opportunities. Help SISTERS Clubs take over the world!

Go to:

WWW.SISTERSRETIREMENT.COM

to find a **SISTERS** club near you!

REFERENCES:

1 "The Top 10 Facts About the Wage Gap," Center for American Progress. http://www.americanprogress.org/issues/labor/news/2012/04/16/11391/the-top-10-facts-about-the-wage-gap/.

2 Ibid.

Chapter 11

Step Seven:
How to Count Your Money
for Fun and Profit

It is said that Mahatma Gandhi was able to accomplish so much because he was congruent in his thoughts, words, and actions. There is a famous story about Gandhi that goes like this:

There once was a mother who was dismayed that her son ate so much sugar. No matter how much she cajoled him, she could not get him to stop. She decided she would take her son to see the great Master Mahatma Gandhi, who would surely cure her son of his sugar addiction. They walked for hours in the scorching sun, and when they finally arrived and stood before Gandhi, the mother told him about her son's sugar obsession. Gandhi listened intently and then told them to return in two weeks. Two weeks later, the mother and son once more walked for hours in the scorching sun to see Gandhi.

This time Gandhi spoke directly to the son. "Boy, you should stop eating sugar. It is not good for your health." Confused, the woman asked Gandhi why he couldn't have said that two weeks ago. Gandhi replied, "Mother, two weeks ago, I myself was eating too much sugar."

Recognizing myself in that story, I have been humbled into organizing my own financial paperwork before I could tell you to organize yours. Writing this chapter has helped me get organized in counting and keeping track of my own finances.

Counting your money should be fun and easy. For some of us, this comes naturally. For others, it is fraught with many different emotions. There is a technique to counting your money that most of us were never taught. Fortunately, it is a skill we can learn.

Cash flow is the river of life—financially speaking. Cash flow is like a stream of money that either flows to you or away from you. This entire book is about how to get more cash to *come in* to your life. That is why it is called *income*. And as more and more cash flows into your life, you need to keep track of it by counting it. There is an old adage that says anything you measure, or count, is more likely to improve. And that applies particularly to money.

Counting your money is more fun (and easier) when there is more cash flowing *in* than cash flowing *out*. With time and practice, your skill at counting your money will get better, and your money situation will likely improve.

Start by clearing and organizing your workspace. You want your space to be light, inviting, and happy. Clear away clutter and surround yourself with delightful pictures, candles, colors, and flowers. This is a space that you will be using often, so you want it to be inviting and charming.

Organize your paperwork. Clear out and dedicate a drawer for your financial paperwork, so that it is always neat and accessible. That way, you can get a lot done in a small amount of time, without having to clean up and search for your papers every time you want to count your money.

Clear out a second larger drawer for your files. Organize your files according to your tax categories, not by months. This will take a few minutes in the beginning to set up, but it will save you a lot of time as you proceed.

Set up a system for your mail and bills. Open your mail as soon as you receive it. File it immediately. If it is a bill, put it with your bills to be paid. Sit down regularly to pay your bills. Some people like to pay their bills as soon as they receive them. Others pay their bills on a weekly or monthly schedule. Do not go longer than a month without paying all of your bills. Avoid throwing bills carelessly into a drawer. If you don't have enough money to pay your bills in full, write on the bill or envelope the minimum and maximum amount due with the due date. As you get better at counting your money, your bills will become more organized and easier to pay in full.

Change your self-image. See yourself as financially in control instead of financially out of control and fearful. Visualize yourself paying off all your bills and amassing great amounts of money to count. Be positive and optimistic. Circumstances can change quickly for the better. Be hopeful and expect good things to come into your life, including money.

As a rule, do not spend your principal savings. It is too hard to amass savings. One of the quickest ways to create savings is to pay yourself first. Set aside 10 percent of all the income you receive and put it into savings. If you can't manage 10 percent, save at least 1 percent to establish the habit. When your cash flow improves, bump up your savings rate.

Count your money more frequently in the beginning—at least every week. Use your financial statements from your checking account and credit cards to record your spending. Keep a daily spending log for a week or a month to see where you can be more financially efficient. Here is an example of a spending log in the form of a basic spreadsheet.

SPENDING LOG

Month _____ Year _____

	A	B	C	D	E	F	G	H	I	J	K	L	M	N	O	P	Q	R	S	T
	Date	Payee	Save	Cash	Business	House	Food	Utilities	Insurance	Children	Car	Charitiy	Health	Beauty	Clothing	Fun	Debt	Taxes	Other	TOTAL
1																				
2																				
3																				
4																				
5																				
6																				
7																				
8																				
9																				
10																				
11																				
12																				
13																				
14																				
15																				
16																				
17																				
18																				
19																				
20	TOTAL																			

You can create your own spending log, of course, but this will give you an idea of how to get started.

Use technology to your advantage. Set up online access to your accounts for ease, transparency, and current account information. Go online daily in the beginning and monitor your primary checking account—the one you use to pay your bills. Also, go online daily and monitor your credit card accounts if you are actively using them. This should be easy for you since you go online daily to check your emails. Get in the habit.

Sign up for bill-pay with your bank. Set up your bills to be paid the day after your paycheck is deposited into your account. Utilize your bank's website to help organize your finances and investments. Take advantage of other software or online websites to help you organize. Set up spreadsheets for your finances.

Next, set up a spending plan. Use your checkbook and credit card statements to help fill in your spending. As you pay your bills, fill in the spreadsheet by month. On the following page is an example of what a spending plan might look like.

SPENDING LOG

Month _____ Year _____

	A	B	C	D	E	F	G	H	I
1	CATEGORY	PLANNED	WEEK 1	WEEK 2	WEEK 3	WEEK 4	WEEK 5	TOTAL	DIFFERENCE
2	Mortgage/Rent								
3	Home Insurance								
4	Home Maintenance								
5	Taxes								
6	Car								
7	Car Insurance								
8	Car Maintenance								
9	Groceries								
10	Electric								
11	Gas								
12	Water								
13	Heat								
14	Cable								
15	Phone								
16	Medical								
17	Healthclubs/Sports								
18	Personal Grooming								
19	Entertainment								
20	Travel/Leisure								
21	Education								
22	Childcare								
23	Clothing								
24	Charity								
25	Gifts								
26	Credit Cards								
27	Savings								
28	Retirement Savings								
29	Cash Spending								
30	Other								
31	Other								
32	TOTAL								

If you are not computer savvy, on the following page is a paper version that you can copy twelve times and use one for each month.

THE EASY BUDGET

INCOME	Month	Year
Salary or Wages (take home)	_____	_____
Dividends, Interest	_____	_____
Alimony, Child Support	_____	_____
Pension	_____	_____
Social Security	_____	_____
Other_____	_____	_____
Other_____	_____	_____
TOTAL INCOME	_____	_____

EXPENSES		
Mortgage or Rent	_____	_____
2nd Mortgage	_____	_____
Car Payment	_____	_____
Childcare	_____	_____
Utilities, Miscellaneous	_____	_____
Electric	_____	_____
Gas	_____	_____
Water	_____	_____
Heat	_____	_____
Cable	_____	_____
Phone	_____	_____
Food	_____	_____
Taxes	_____	_____
Insurance	_____	_____
Medical	_____	_____
Household Miscellaneous	_____	_____
Clothing	_____	_____
Entertainment, Vacation	_____	_____
Gifts	_____	_____
Credit Card _____	_____	_____
Credit Card _____	_____	_____
Credit Card _____	_____	_____
Credit Card _____	_____	_____
All Store Credit Cards	_____	_____
Charity	_____	_____
Other Expense	_____	_____
Other Expense	_____	_____
TOTAL EXPENSES	_____	_____

TOTAL INCOME MINUS
TOTAL EXPENSES EQUALS

SAVING (DIS-SAVING) _____ _____

Keep a yearly master budget. As each month is completed, add that month's expenses to your yearly master budget.

Master Budget
Year _____

A	B	C	D	E	F	G	H	I	J	K	L	M	N
	JAN	FEB	MAR	APR	MAY	JUNE	JULY	AUG	SEPT	OCY	NOV	DEC	TOTAL
1 YEAR 20___													
2 Savings													
3 Cash													
4 Business													
5 Household													
6 Food													
7 Utilities													
8 Insurance													
9 Children													
10 Car													
11 Charities													
12 Health													
13 Beauty													
14 Clothing													
15 Fun													
16 Debt Reduction													
17 Taxes													
18 Other													
19 Other													
20													
21 TOTAL													

QUICK FIXES FOR A BROKEN BUDGET

1. *Budget.* The very word "budget" feels like the word "diet"—potentially rewarding but not much fun in the application! However, if your weight is out of control, chances are you need a diet. The same would apply to your money: if your spending is out of control, you probably need a budget, also known as a spending plan. How do you want to spend your money? Plan for it.

2. *Change your mindset.* Take responsibility and control. Even if you have never done a budget or paid the bills before, maintain a "can-do" attitude. Don't let yourself become overwhelmed, and don't let fear slow you down.

3. *Keep a spending log for one month.* Record your spending in a small notebook, in the sample Monthly Spending form, or on your smartphone. You'll be amazed to see where your dollars go.

4. *Reduce expenses.* Once you have done a spending log and a budget, analyze your household finances to see where you can reduce expenses.

Eliminate subscriptions and memberships that you no longer need. Slow down the frequency of appointments for personal maintenance. Shop for clothes in your own closet.

5. *Choose your options.* A budget really means, "How I choose to spend my money." If you want to buy those expensive designer shoes, go ahead. Just make an off-setting choice in another part of your budget—for example, you may choose to do your own nails for a month or two, or to brown bag your lunch for a while.

6. *Create additional income from employment.* Get a second job if necessary. Use the income from your second job to pay off credit cards, school loans, or HELOCs.

7. *Refinance your home mortgage to a lower rate.* If you can refinance to a lower rate, you could possibly free up hundreds of dollars per month or more, which could greatly help balance your finances.

8. *Downsize your home.* One of the fastest ways to balance a budget is to downsize to a smaller home or apartment with less overhead.

9. *Consider non-traditional living arrangements.* If you have extra rooms, consider renting them out, or getting a roommate. Rent out your garage or vacation home.

10. *Optimize the return on your investments without taking on excessive risk.* Many of us have too much savings in cash that provides very little interest. Consider moving some of your cash into a high quality, short-term bond fund.

11. *Have a fire sale.* Sell unwanted clutter through online auction sites, or have an old-fashioned yard sale. Sell extraneous electronic devices, old textbooks, designer clothes, furniture, cars, baby items, etc.

12. *Balance volunteerism with paid work.* Women are admirable for the amount of hours we give to volunteering. However, unless you are independently wealthy, keep volunteer time in balance with paid time. You need income!

13. *Devise creative solutions.* Consider ways you can share costs with co-workers or friends, such as sharing a business office and/or secretary if you are self-employed. Create a carpool to share

transportation costs. Trade babysitting duties with other moms to reduce childcare costs.

14. *Pay yourself first.* You need to have an emergency fund of at least nine to twelve months' living expenses. You might put three months' worth into CDs and the rest into high-quality short-term bond funds. Set aside the first 10 percent of everything you earn to build your emergency fund.

15. *Meet with a financial advisor.* She may be able to provide meaningful insights and suggestions, and the first meeting is often free.

16. *Respect yourself more.* When you respect yourself more, you take better care of yourself, your health, and your money. When you respect yourself, you become respectable.

WHAT'S FUN ABOUT COUNTING YOUR MONEY?

This may be the best part yet. Counting your money can be really fun if, when you do so, you feel like you are getting richer! Income from employment is easy to count. And isn't it fun when you get a raise! Now you're counting your money!

You are getting richer when your assets—what you own—are growing and your liabilities—what you owe—are shrinking. For example, when you save in your 401(k), your assets are growing, and when you pay down your mortgage, credit cards, or school loan, your liabilities are shrinking. When this happens, all other things being equal, you are increasing your net worth, which means—getting richer.

Counting your money is fun as you feel more in control, more confident, and increasingly sure of yourself. You'll watch your net worth increase month by month, creating more financial options for yourself. Eventually you'll realize you no longer have to panic or worry at the end of the month—you can relax and breathe more easily because you have created far-reaching freedoms and a liberating lifestyle.

On the following page is a spreadsheet to help you measure your net worth by keeping track of your assets and liabilities.

WOMEN, MONEY & PROSPERITY

	JANUARY 20____	APRIL 20____	JULY 20____	OCTOBER 20____
ASSETS				
Checking				
Savings				
401(k)				
403(b)				
457 Plan				
Profit Sharing Plan				
Deferred Compensation				
IRA				
Brokerage Account				
Dividend Reinvestment Plans				
Trusts				
Whole Life Insurance				
Mineral Rights				
Primary Residence				
Rental Property				
Vacation Property				
Gold, Jewelry, Art				
Vehicles				
Other				
TOTAL ASSETS				
LIABILITIES				
Mortgage 1				
Mortgage 2				
HELOC				
School Loan				
Car Loan				
Credit Card 1				
Credit Card 2				
All Store Cards				
Other				
TOTAL LIABILITIES				
NET WORTH = Total Assets-Total Liabilities				
TOTAL NET WORTH				

SAMPLE ASSETS AND LIABILITIES

	JANUARY 20____	APRIL 20____	JULY 20____	OCTOBER 20____
ASSETS				
Checking	5000	5000	5000	5000
Savings	12500	12600	12700	12800
401(k)	72000	72500	73000	73500
403(b)				
457 Plan				
Profit Sharing Plan				
Deferred Compensation				
IRA	39000	39100	39200	39300
Brokerage Account	10000	10100	10200	10300
Dividend Reinvestment Plans	8000	8050	8100	8150
Trusts				
Whole Life Insurance				
Mineral Rights				
Primary Residence	250000	250000	250000	250000
Rental Property	150000	150000	150000	150000
Vacation Property				
Gold, Jewelry, Art				
Vehicles	25000	24500	24000	23500
Other				
TOTAL ASSETS	**571500**	**571850**	**572200**	**572550**
LIABILITIES				
Mortgage 1	187500	186100	184750	183300
Mortgage 2	120000	119500	119000	118550
HELOC				
School Loan				
Car Loan	15000	13800	12650	11400
Credit Card 1				
Credit Card 2				
All Store Cards				
Other				
TOTAL LIABILITIES	**322500**	**319400**	**316400**	**313250**
NET WORTH = Total Assets-Total Liabilities				
TOTAL NET WORTH	**249000**	**252450**	**255800**	**259300**

This becomes more and more fun every month as you watch the improvement in your financial situation. Don't get discouraged if at first it seems like only a small improvement or even if it's going in the wrong direction. We all start somewhere, and once you make a start, you can make an improvement. Be consistent in regularly—monthly or quarterly—adding up all your assets and liabilities. The important thing is to watch the trend: if the trend is improving, your net worth is growing. Even if only slightly, you are succeeding. Persevere!

HOW TO COUNT YOUR INVESTMENT MONEY FOR FUN OR PROFIT

I've already discussed how to measure total return from an investment.

Total Return % = The dollar amount the stock, bond or mutual fund goes up (or down), plus the dividend or interest, divided by the original investment amount

It's also fun to watch the value of your investments go up. This is another form of counting your money for fun and profit. One of the best ways to do this is to use technology to your advantage. Most bank and brokerage firms' websites help you easily keep track of your investments. Or you can utilize other websites or software that is specifically designed to help you track your investments.

INVESTMENTS

	A	B	C	D	E	F	G	H	I	J	K
	DATE	INVESTMENT	QUANTITY	LOCATION	ACCOUNT TYPE	PURCHASE DATE	COST	DIVIDEND/ INTEREST DATE	DIVIDEND/ INTEREST AMOUNT	CURRENT MARKET VALUE	GAIN/(LOSS)
1											
2											
3											
4											
5											
6											
7											
8											
9											
10											
11											
12											
13											
14											
15											
16											
17											
18											
19											
20											
21											

For those who prefer to keep track of their investments manually, here is an investment worksheet.

HOW TO COUNT YOUR SMALL BUSINESS MONEY FOR FUN OR PROFIT

If you decide to start a small business, counting your business money is essential. One reason that many small businesses fail is because the business owner fails to or does not know how to count her business money. If you are creating a small business and don't know how to keep books or count your business money, here are some remedies:

- Connect with a business partner who has good accounting skills
- Consult your CPA and/or financial advisor
- Hire a retired or part-time bookkeeper
- Utilize accounting software programs, such as QuickBooks
- Read books on accounting to increase your financial literacy
- Read financial newspapers so you get familiar with the terms
- Go to www.sba.gov to learn about business and financial topics

Chapter 12

How Much Do You Need?
How Much Can You Spend?
(And What I Would Tell My Sister)

This chapter is the reason I wrote this book—for my sisters and for all the women who are trying to figure out their own retirement plan. By the time you read this and start to plan and save for retirement, you may discover that you are already behind, that you should have started years ago, that you feel you can't possibly save enough for what you need by the time you retire.

Save anyway.

IT'S NOT YOUR FAULT

There are many circumstances beyond your control, many reasons why it is not your fault if you are not where you would like to be in your retirement planning. I have explained these factors in previous chapters, but I will list them again here:

- A lifetime of lower earnings
  . . . which meant little or no discretionary
  funds to save for retirement
- Not getting equivalent job promotions
  . . . which meant not getting executive
  retirement benefits
- Working in jobs that don't offer pensions
  and retirement benefits
- Leaving the workforce to care for children
  and parents
  . . . which contributed to lower pay and fewer
  promotions
  . . . which also contributed to lower Social
  Security benefits
- Spending your resources (time, money, and
  energy) on childcare and eldercare instead of
  on your own retirement saving
- Incurring higher per capita living expenses if
  you are a single woman, (single, divorced, or
  widowed) living on your own, thereby draining your ability to save for retirement
- Failure of our education system to teach
  financial literacy

And then there are the non-quantifiable factors,
such as lower self-esteem that many women feel. This

can hold women back from asking for what they need, such as a pay raise, or the courage to call a financial advisor to ask for a consultation.

GETTING TO SAFE

If you are like many women, you have spent much of your adult life just trying to get to that safe place about money. *You just wanted to feel safe!* You wanted to breathe easy and know that there would always be enough to pay your bills at the end of the month *without worrying.* If you're like millions of other women, you've taken care of everyone else—your spouse, your kids, your parents, tuition, mortgage, weddings—and now that it's your turn, *you just want to feel safe about your retirement.* It's that old "bag-lady" fear that all women understand and men don't experience.

THE DEVIL YOU KNOW

Most women don't know how much they need for retirement or how much they can spend once they are in retirement. I present the information here, not to scare you, but so that you have factual information about your own retirement planning. *Do not get discouraged if the numbers seem daunting. I will lead you back into the light, with some ideas on how to fix your own retirement plan. I promise.*

Here goes.

HOW MUCH DO YOU NEED FOR RETIREMENT?

Calculating how much you need for retirement can be a challenge. It entails numerous scenarios with many variables, such as age at retirement, rate of return on your portfolio, the withdrawal rate (to fund your spending needs), market behavior, inflation, age at death, and luck.

Author Jim C. Otar, CFP, CMT, BASc, MEng, has a background in engineering and a talent for mathematical problems. In his book, *Unveiling the Retirement Myth: Advanced Retirement Planning Based on Market History*, he provides invaluable charts to help us understand the mathematics of money and retirement planning.

Otar has developed the *asset multiplier*, which is "the dollar amount of money required at the beginning of retirement for each dollar of lifelong withdrawal, indexed in subsequent years for inflation."[1] The age of death is assumed to be ninety-five, because it provides "between 5 percent and 15 percent survival rate,"[2] (or, likelihood you will keep living).

To explain this chart: for someone retiring at age sixty-five, whose portfolio had a 4 percent annual growth rate and a 3 percent inflation rate, the asset multiplier would be 25. We'll use this in the following example.

Asset Multiplier for a Portfolio with a steady 4% Annual Growth Rate			
RETIREMENT AGE	AT 2% INFLATION	AT 3% INFLATION	AT 4% INFLATION
55	27.0	32.3	38.5
60	24.4	28.6	33.3
65	22.2	25.0	28.6
70	19.2	21.3	23.8
75	16.1	17.5	19.2

Let's say you had a portfolio that provided a steady 4 percent growth rate, inflation was 3 percent, and you wanted to retire at age sixty-five and withdraw $20,000 per year. Here is Jim Otar's formula to figure out how much you need to have saved:

$$\text{Savings Required} = \text{\$ Amount Withdrawn at Start of Retirement} \times \text{Asset Multiplier}$$

$$\text{\$500,000} = \text{\$20,000} \times 25$$

So at age sixty-five, in a 3 percent inflation environment, if you wanted to withdraw $20,000 annually for thirty years (to meet your spending needs) from a portfolio that had a steady 4 percent growth rate, you would need to have saved $500,000.

What if in this same scenario you delayed retirement to age seventy? From the above chart we can see that the asset multiplier at age seventy is 21.3.

$426,000 = $20,000 x 21.3

At age seventy, you would only need $426,000 to withdraw $20,000 annually from a 4 percent growth portfolio in a 3 percent inflation environment. The difference is that you would only withdraw funds for twenty-five years, from age seventy to ninety-five.

Here is how different withdrawal amounts affect the savings you will need at age sixty-five with a 4 percent growth portfolio in a 3 percent inflation rate environment:

Savings Required at 65	= $ Withdrawal Amount	x Asset Multiplier (3% Inflation)
$250,000	$10,000	25
$500,000	$20,000	25
$625,000	$25,000	25
$750,000	$30,000	25
$875,000	$35,000	25
$1,000,000	$40,000	25

So in this example, if you wanted to withdraw (and spend) $10,000 every year throughout the thirty years of your retirement (ages sixty-five to ninety-five), you would need to have saved $250,000.

The following shows how waiting until age seventy to retire can make a huge difference in what you will need to have saved, given the same 4 percent growth portfolio and 3 percent inflation rate.

Savings Required at 70	= $ Withdrawal Amount	x Asset Multiplier (3% Inflation)
$213,000	$10,000	21.3
$426,000	$20,000	21.3
$532,500	$25,000	21.3
$639,000	$30,000	21.3
$745,500	$35,000	21.3
$852,000	$40,000	21.3

So in this example, if you wanted to withdraw (and spend) $10,000 every year throughout the twenty-five years of your retirement (ages seventy to ninety-five), you would only need to have saved $213,000.

Beware

If inflation is higher, you will need to save much more. For a woman with a 4 percent growth portfolio who wanted to start retirement at age sixty-five in a *4 percent inflation* environment, the asset multiplier is 28.6. Let's see how that plays out.

Savings Required at 65	= $ Withdrawal Amount	x Asset Multiplier (4% Inflation)
$286,000	$10,000	28.6
$572,000	$20,000	28.6
$715,000	$25,000	28.6
$858,000	$30,000	28.6
$1,001,000	$35,000	28.6
$1,144,000	$40,000	28.6

So in this example of higher inflation (4 percent rate), if you wanted to withdraw (and spend) $10,000 every year for the thirty years of your retirement (ages sixty-five to ninety-five), you would need to have saved $286,000.

What if you could get a higher return, or growth rate, on your portfolio? If you could achieve a hypothetical 6 percent annual return on your portfolio, that would change the asset multiplier.

Asset Multiplier for a Portfolio with a steady 6% Annual Growth Rate			
RETIREMENT AGE	AT 2% INFLATION	AT 3% INFLATION	AT 4% INFLATION
55	19.6	23.3	26.3
60	18.5	21.3	24.4
65	17.2	19.2	21.7
70	15.4	16.9	18.9
75	13.3	14.5	15.9

So how much would you need to have saved at age sixty-five if you had a 6 percent growth portfolio in a 3 percent inflation environment and you wanted to withdraw $10,000 annually?

Savings Required	=	$ Withdrawal Amount	x	Asset Multiplier at 6% Growth, 3% Inflation
$192,000	=	$10,000	x	19.2

So in this example of a higher growth portfolio (6 percent), if you wanted to withdraw and spend $10,000 every year for the thirty years of your retirement (ages sixty-five to ninety-five), you would need to have saved $192,000—assuming you could achieve a steady 6 percent return on your portfolio.

Is a 6 percent average annual return (growth rate on your portfolio) feasible? Let's put this in perspective. Markets fluctuate greatly from year to year. The average annual growth rate of the Dow Jones Industrial Average (DJIA)—a blue chip stock market indicator—between 1900–2004 was 7.3 percent.[3] However, the median return was 3.7 percent. That means that half of the time the market was above a 3.7 percent growth rate, and half the time it was below a 3.7 percent growth rate.

Otar believes that it is not the average annual return that is important. "During the savings, or accumulation stage (before you retire), the most important thing is the *volatility of returns*. During the spending, or distribution stage (after you retire), the most important thing is the *sequence of returns*."[4]

Let's say that during the thirty years of your retirement, you are withdrawing at a conservative 4 percent rate, and half the time the market is above 3.7 percent median growth, and half the time it is below 3.7 percent median growth. If all the below 3.7 percent median growth rate market returns occur in the first fifteen years of your retirement, and all the above 3.7 percent median growth rate market returns occur in the last fifteen years, you are very likely to deplete your portfolio of investments in the early years of your retirement because of a bad sequence of market returns. This is known as "statistically unlucky." Indeed!

Otar's data suggests that during the accumulation (savings) phase, you might consider using a 60 percent equity (stocks)/40 percent fixed income (bond) asset allocation to provide positive returns with less volatility. During the distribution (spending) phase, consider using a 40 percent equity/60 percent fixed income asset allocation for the least likelihood of portfolio depletion.[5]

HOW MUCH CAN YOU SPEND IN RETIREMENT?

Ideally, after allowing for our legacy and estate goals, we would like to spend as much as we want in retirement—have the most fun!—and not run out of money. The retirement time of our lives is known as the *distribution phase*, because we are making *distributions* of our own savings to ourselves throughout the course of our retirement for our living expenses.

So, how much can you spend in retirement? Normally, we take a certain percentage of our total savings and investments every year to live on. This is known as the *distribution rate* or *withdrawal rate*. At what rate will you withdraw money from your portfolio of savings and investments to fund your living expenses?

The one question to ask yourself is, "Do you have enough assets so that you can live off of just the interest on your investments, or will you need to spend down your principal?"

Let's say, hypothetically, that you have $1 million in a tax-free bond that pays you 4 percent interest income. This bond would pay you $40,000 (tax-free) per year.

$1,000,000 x .04 = $40,000 per year

That might be enough for you to live on without touching the principal—especially if you were to stack this income stream (the bond interest) on top of your Social Security and pension or other investment income.

However, let's say that you had only $200,000 in that same tax-free bond which pays 4 percent tax-free income. In that case, you would earn $8,000 per year.

$200,000 x .04 = $8,000 per year

That may not be enough to live on, even when you add in Social Security. At some point, you may need to spend down your principal. But at what rate should you spend your principal to ensure that it lasts your lifetime without causing you to run out of money? What is a safe withdrawal rate?

The conventional wisdom has been to use an initial withdrawal rate, indexed for inflation, of 4 percent. Studies have shown that, starting at age sixty-five, if your initial withdraw rate is 4 percent of your portfolio, indexed for inflation every year, you would have a high likelihood of not outliving your money.[6] Theoretically, if you could earn a 7 percent average after-tax return on your portfolio, and if inflation averaged 3 percent, and you withdrew your funds at 4 percent, your savings would remain constant and you would not outlive your money.

One cautionary note, as we have just discovered, is that planning for "average" portfolio return, "average" inflation, "average" tax rates, or even "average" withdrawal rates from your portfolio can be dangerous. Economic recessions throw averages off and destroy even the best retirement plan assumptions. This can derail even the most carefully constructed retirement plan. Economic output (GDP), stock markets, portfolio returns, inflation, and spending needs all fluctuate.

One recent theory of retirement spending is to use a variable withdrawal rate. For example, if the economy and stock market are doing well, then use an initial withdrawal rate (indexed for inflation) of, say, 4 percent. If the economy is in recession or the stock market is down, use a smaller withdrawal rate of, say, 2 percent to 2.5 percent. When you withdraw your principal from the market when the market is down, you lock in a permanent loss, and also lose future earnings power on the money that is now lost. Still, reducing spending in a recession can be difficult.

Another approach would be to start with the least percentage amount you could afford to live on, say, 1 to 2 percent, and gradually increase that percentage rate to cap out at, say, 4 percent, depending on your age, portfolio size, and other factors.

One strategy, according to Otar, is to transfer two years' worth of withdrawal funds into a money market, an additional three years' worth of withdrawals into a short-term bond fund, and the rest into equities. Then make your withdrawals from the money market. When rebalancing, be sure to replenish the money market first.[7] However, if you move funds from the stock market into the money market for this purpose when the market is down, you will still be locking in a loss.

So the question becomes, can you forestall starting your retirement and taking withdrawals until the economy is robust and the stock market positive? This may require you to delay the start of your retirement withdrawals by anywhere from one to five years, to allow the economy to recover from a recession and the market to regain some of its losses. Difficult as this might be, it would have a very positive effect on the success of your retirement spending plan. In other words, it would greatly improve the chances that you would not run out of money.

WITHDRAWAL RATE (A.K.A. SPENDING RATE)

Jim C. Otar says that "the withdrawal rate is the most important contributor of portfolio longevity. It is far more important than asset allocation, asset selection, management fees, dividends, and reverse dollar cost averaging. A seemingly small increase in withdrawals can change the outcome drastically."[8] Let me emphasize this: *how much you spend each year in retirement is the most important factor of all, and even a slight increase in spending may derail your retirement plan success.*

He goes on to define the *sustainable withdrawal rate* (SWR) as "the maximum amount of money one can withdraw from a retirement portfolio on a periodic basis with no probability of depleting these savings during one's lifetime. It is based on market history and expressed as a percentage of portfolio value."[9] In actual practice, however, the sustainable withdrawal rates Otar provides incorporate a 90 percent probability of portfolio survival (not running out of money), and a

10 percent possibility of portfolio depletion (running out of money).

Here is a chart of Otar's simplified sustainable withdrawal rates.

TIME HORIZON	SUSTAINABLE WITHDRAWAL RATE (USA)
20 Years	5.2%
30 Years	3.8%
40 Years	3.1%

So if you retired at age sixty-five, you would be able to use a 3.8 percent withdrawal rate from your portfolio and have a 90 percent probability of not running out of money by age ninety-five. Otar warns against rounding up the 3.8 percent rate to an even 4 percent, as even the slightest deviation can negatively impact your retirement plan. If you spend less than the sustainable withdrawal rate (in this case, less than 3.8 percent), your portfolio would actually grow over time.

Here is a chart of Otar's *sustainable asset multipliers (SAM)*, which shows how much money you would need to have saved for $10,000 annual income, fully indexed to CPI (inflation) over the course of your retirement. I include it because inflation is a critical factor in your retirement plan, particularly in the later years of your retirement.

TIME HORIZON	MINIMUM PORTFOLIO (SAVINGS) REQUIRED FOR $10,000 ANNUAL INCOME, FULLY INDEXED FOR CPI
20 Years	$192,300
30 Years	$263,200
40 Years	$322,600

In other words, if you retired at age sixty-five, and wanted to spend $10,000 per year for the next thirty years until age ninety-five, after taking into account the effects of annual inflation, you would need $263,200.[10]

If you want to know what your own withdrawal rate or expected withdrawal rate is, divide your initial (first year's) withdrawal amount in dollars by your total savings.

$$\text{Withdrawal Rate} = \frac{\text{Initial Withdrawal Amount in Dollars}}{\text{Total Investment Portfolio}}$$

$$6\% = \frac{\$60,000}{\$1,000,000}$$

$$3.8\% = \frac{\$38,000}{\$1,000,000}$$

$$3.8\% = \frac{\$19,000}{\$500,000}$$

If you had $1,000,000 saved for retirement and you withdrew $60,000 in the first year, that would mean that your withdrawal rate is 6 percent. A 3.8 percent withdrawal rate would mean that you could withdraw $38,000 from your $1,000,000 investment portfolio every year and be reasonably sure of having enough assets throughout your lifetime. If you had $500,000 saved for retirement, a 3.8 percent withdrawal rate would mean that you could spend $19,000 per year and be reasonably confident that you would not run out of money in retirement.

If your withdrawal rate is over 3.8 percent, Otar believes that you should export some of your retirement income risk—which is the risk of not having enough retirement income—to an insurance company with an annuity product that will pay you income for life and will be indexed fully for inflation. An insurance company can guarantee a higher rate of return because they pool their risk over large numbers of insured persons.

If you have enough money and assets in your portfolio that your withdrawal rate is 3.8 percent or less, celebrate! You are in Otar's "green zone"—no worries! You will most likely have an abundant retirement.

If your withdrawal rate is between 4 percent and 5 percent, your portfolio is expected to last you about twenty years. That's probably all right if you retire at age seventy-five, but less sure if you retire at an age younger than seventy-five. You are in Otar's gray zone of uncertainty as to whether or not you will have sufficient assets to last throughout your retirement.

If your initial withdrawal rate at age sixty-five is 6 percent, chances are strong that you are retiring too young. It is very unlikely that your funds will last throughout the thirty years of your retirement. You are in Otar's "red zone." Stop and rethink your actions. Delaying retirement even for a few years can make a big difference.

If your withdrawal rate or expected withdrawal rate is greater than 3.8 percent, find a good financial advisor to help guide you—sooner rather than later. Reevaluate your budget and spending plan. Can you eliminate the non-essential items?

Resist gifting or loaning money to children, grandchildren, charities, and other worthy causes, especially in the early years of retirement. You can give to your loved ones in your trust (or will). Instead of putting yourself in a position where you will be dependent on your children in your old age, you can give them the gift of an inheritance, and a loving memory of you. Preserve as much of your money for as long as you can.

Take heart. Be optimistic. Most pre-retirees—and pensions—are underfunded. Thankfully, you still have time to employ new strategies for retirement success—if you act now. Let's discuss some retirement solutions.

A NEW APPROACH

When I researched the facts about retirement for women, I was amazed. By the time women get around to focusing on their own retirement, it seems almost too late for them to save enough. (Save anyway—you will be glad you did.)

That is why I wrote this book. I knew we needed to take a very different approach. That approach is all the action steps I have described in this book. And these steps can lead you out of the darkness of fear, into the light of confidence and ease, through successful retirement strategies. Again, they are these:

- Create several Stackable Income Streams To Empower Retirement Security
- Always Be Earning (ABE)
- Use the abundant time you still have to earn and invest
- Delay your retirement start date
- Work part-time
- Pool your assets with like-minded women to create business opportunities
- Create a home-based business with positive cash flow, using the talents you already have (Note: negative cash flow will be a drag on your retirement.)
- Share expenses
- Use non-traditional living tactics, such as renting out rooms of your home

- Get a roommate
- Downsize your home to a less expensive abode
- Create income from a rental property with positive cash flow (Note: negative cash flow will be a drag on your retirement.)
- Become financially literate
- Consider exporting some of your retirement income risk to an annuity that is fully indexed for inflation
- Delay taking Social Security benefits; or, take spousal benefits first, then take yours later, when they are higher; if your spouse is deceased, you may be entitled to survivor benefits; consult with Social Security first before you make a decision about your benefits
- Research Medicare at www.medicare.gov and don't miss the age-sixty-five sign-up date; consult an insurance agent who specializes in Medicare plans
- Value your credit, and if necessary, work to improve it
- Pay off unproductive debt (credit cards, HELOCs, etc.)
- Rework your budget and spending plan; eliminate non-essentials
- Research your own retirement

- Do a retirement plan on yourself
- Meet with a financial advisor
- Talk about retirement with your friends
- Start a SISTERS club.

SAFETY IN NUMBERS

When I was a young woman and wanted to go out to socialize, my mom always told me to find a few friends to go out with. She said there was "safety in numbers." I would like to suggest that as we women approach retirement—now, more than ever, there is still safety in numbers.

As a group, women are an economic force. Together, women are a powerful catalyst for financial success—if we would network as a community and connect. We could raise the economic well-being of all women if we supported each other, bought from each other, sold to each other, financed each other, and did business with each other.

A recent program launched by Goldman Sachs known as "10,000 Women" showed that by raising the income of women, even at the lowest level, the entire community benefited and the resulting projection is that it would actually raise the GDP (gross domestic product) of the entire world.[11]

Start your own community of women who are willing to take responsibility and claim their power over their own retirement. Communicate with women about retirement. Let's start a grassroots conversation, a grass-fire. Let's go viral about retirement planning for women of all ages. Start a SISTERS club; enlist a few friends who care enough about their own retirement to take action. Get started *now* to create Several Stackable Income Streams To Empower Retirement Security. Create economic well-being for all women by creating economic strength in yourself. And share your retirement success stories at www.sistersretirement. com. I want to hear from you.

REFERENCES:

1 Otar, Jim C. *Unveiling the Retirement Myth: Advanced Retirement Planning Based on Market History*. Otar & Associates: 2009, p. 29.

2 Ibid, p. 177.

3 Ibid, p. 33.

4 Ibid, p. 59.

5 Ibid, p. 160-162.

6 http://www.gao.gov/assets/320/319390.html.

7 Otar, Jim C. *Unveiling the Retirement Myth: Advanced Retirement Planning Based on Market History*. Otar & Associates: 2009, p. 163-165.

8 Ibid, p. 177.

9 Ibid, p. 180.

10 Ibid, p. 188.

11 "10,000 Women," Goldman Sachs. http://www.goldmansachs.com/citizenship/10000women/index.html.

Chapter 13

Living Your Values

A well-planned retirement should be a time of freedom, abundance, enjoyment, personal fulfillment, travel, special occasions with loved ones, and peace of mind. By planning and getting organized well in advance—at least five to ten years—you will then be able to relax and enjoy a carefree retirement.

While you are still working and have income, think about all the deferred maintenance projects you will need to address. Perhaps you will need a new roof or garage door. Sprucing up your surroundings for retirement creates a positive, happy environment.

Large remodeling projects just before or after retirement, however, can be problematic. The reason is that they have a tendency to become much larger and cost much more than you think they will, and then start to eat into your retirement savings. Fund your projects out of your work income before you retire without impinging on your retirement savings schedule. Also, before you retire, set aside funds for large purchases, such as a car or a big trip.

For some people, sudden retirement comes as a shock, even if they have plenty of money. They are at a loss as to how they should spend their time and money. They are not sure what they are "supposed to be doing." Some feel lost without the structure of a work schedule and a social circle of long-time work friends. You may want to consider gradually scaling into retirement over two to five years.

WHAT DO YOU VALUE?

By the time you get to retirement, you realize that there are some things in life that are important, and some that are not. In your planning stage, try to identify the things that are important to you. Focus on them and de-clutter the rest of your life.

Value Your Money

Money is an important factor for retirement. With adequate money, you have more options—to travel, live where you want to, buy a new car, maintain your home the way you would like to, plan multi-generational family vacations, and have control over your life. Save more than you think you will need. Keep up a regular monthly budget, so that if you start to overspend your plan, you can catch it early and make course adjustments.

Insurance

Since your money is important, you will want to think about protecting it with insurance. There are numerous kinds of insurance, depending on your needs. Consult an insurance specialist. You will need Medicare, including parts A: with hospitalization and nursing; B: medical insurance; possibly D for prescription drugs; and C for Advantage plans such as HMOs and PPOs (see www. medicare.gov).

Other types of insurance you may want to investigate are whole life, or permanent, insurance to create an estate or offset estate taxes; term insurance to create an estate for a limited time with lower premiums; and long-term care insurance, to cover you in case you need nursing care, either in your home or at a skilled nursing facility. If you own a small business, in whole or in part, there are several types of business insurance that will make it easy to transition ownership of your business to the next generation or your business partners, and still maintain the value of the business. These include *key person* and *buy-sell agreements*.

Estate Planning

The best gift you can give your loved ones is a well-structured estate plan. Talk to your financial advisor about your estate plan. Work with a good estate-planning attorney to get your affairs in order. Do your heirs a big favor and consolidate your accounts into one place. Why make them chase all over town to find assets that you forgot to tell them about?

Simplify your accounts and your paperwork. Make sure everything is titled correctly. Review your beneficiaries and update them after any life-changing financial events, such as a birth, death, divorce, or moving to a different state. Keep an inventory and leave well-written instructions in the form of an estate trust document. If you want your heirs to divide your assets according to your wishes, you have to let them know what your wishes are.

There are five important estate-planning documents you will need:

1. A will
2. A durable power of attorney
3. A durable power of attorney for health care
4. A living will
5. A trust

1. A **will** is a document that gives written instructions on how you would like your assets distributed to your heirs upon your death. You appoint an executor to oversee your affairs, pay your estate taxes and final expenses, and then distribute your assets. If you have children who are minors, a will allows you to designate a guardian. Since a will takes effect at your death, it does not effectively provide for the management of your assets if you become incapacitated. A will must be probated in the courts, which can be time-consuming and costly.

2. A **durable power of attorney** is a document that names a person to act on your behalf. This person is called your agent or attorney-in-fact. You can assign very limited or very broad powers to your agent, who would act on your behalf if you should become incapacitated, or no longer wish to oversee your own affairs. It is not unusual to give your agent the right to buy or sell investments for you, including real estate, and to manage your financial affairs, so make sure this is a person you trust.

3. A **health care power of attorney** is a document that authorizes someone else to make your medical decisions for you in case you cannot. Having such a designated person can help avoid family disputes during challenging medical situations.

4. A **living will** states in writing what your preferences are for medical life support in terminal illness.

5. A **revocable living trust** is a document that provides written instructions for your estate plan. There are many different types of trusts, each with its own special purpose. A revocable living trust has several advantages over a simple will. It is a legal vehicle that enables the management of your financial affairs during your lifetime (if you are incapacitated, for example), at your death, and even throughout generations of heirs to follow. It allows you to avoid probate, and helps protect your privacy by reducing the likelihood that your personal information will be part of the public record.

Every revocable trust has three key roles. The *grantor (or settlor)*—generally, you—creates the trust and funds it by transferring assets to it. The *beneficiaries*—typically you and your family—receive income and/or principal from the trust assets during your lifetime, and then pass according to the instructions of your trust to your heirs at your death. The *trustee* is the person appointed in the trust to manage the assets of the trust. This is typically you, your family or a corporate trustee, such as a bank.[1]

If you do not transfer assets into your revocable living trust, they are considered to be outside the trust, and would have to go through probate. It's one thing to create a trust, but you have to fund it by retitling assets into the name of the trust.

Value Your Health

We've all heard the old adage "Time is money." Now I say, "Health is money." As health care becomes increasingly expensive, I tell clients to give health care a line item (larger consideration) in their household budget—not unlike a mortgage.

One way to keep the cost of health care down is by keeping the state of your own health up. Become proactive now. Don't wait for retirement to improve your health habits—you know the ones: anything that follows the word *excessive*. Excessive eating of calories, fats, salts, sugars and empty carbohydrates, excessive drinking, smoking, etc. We all know who we are.

Then there is the *not enough of*: not enough of quality foods like fruits and veggies, not enough exercise. By exercising regularly and eating a healthy diet, you are much more likely to lose weight and reduce heart disease, high blood pressure, stroke, cholesterol, diabetes, arthritis pain, and more.

Try to lose weight. If you eliminate just 100 calories a day, you will lose ten pounds in a year. That might be as easy as giving up cream in your coffee or switching to low-fat milk. Find a fun form of exercise. If it is something you really enjoy doing, you are more likely to continue with consistency. Enlist a friend in your health regimen. Create a healthy lifestyle together and have fun with it. Get energized!

Consult with your physician to ensure that you are on the right course and taking the right medicines. As you maintain your weight, diet, and health better, you will have fewer doctor visits, fewer procedures, fewer medical bills, and fewer time-outs to address medical issues.

Another benefit of good health is the vitality it gives you to enjoy life more. You will have more energy to keep up with your children and grandchildren or nieces and nephews. And you are less likely to become dependent on them for health care in your older years. Take responsibility, turn over a leaf if necessary, and get control over your health. Your loved ones will thank you. And so will you!

Value Your Community

Before you retire, look around and consider who are the people you will want to spend time with once you retire. It is not unusual to lose touch with your work friends as you separate from daily contact and the commonality of work.

The most obvious community is your family. If you are married, how close are you with your spouse? Do you enjoy each other's company? Do you share any activities? While it is important to create your own sacred space, have you carved out no-fly zone territories in different parts of the house to avoid communication?

This would be a good time to take an honest look at your relationships with your spouse and children. They can be a source of enriching life experience or a disappointing timeline of bland emotions. Now would be a good time to have a heart-to-heart talk, and seek counseling if necessary, to restore, repair, or reinvigorate close family relationships. Why not share the best time of your life with the ones you love the most?

Over time, family members may move apart or become estranged over personality differences, family businesses, or other issues, such as the division of estate assets. It's time to bury the hatchet and reestablish with your family members. When was the last time you called that recalcitrant sibling? Societal expectations are that we will take care of family members in their—our—old age. It behooves all of us to remain on good terms. Develop a close connection with the next generation of nieces, nephews, and grandchildren as well.

Maintain old friendships and create new ones. It takes a little bit of effort to keep up with friends—even when we want to. Make the effort. Look for ways to bring new friends into your life, especially younger friends, who are likely to still be there in your old age.

Do not allow yourself to become isolated in retirement. Isolation can lead to depression, lack of interest in life, a gradual decline in health, and possibly even a loss of control over your affairs. One of the best cures for isolation is to get a pet—yes, even if you're not the pet type. I've seen loving pets transform even the most hardened isolationist. Just think: they love you unconditionally! Who else can you say that about?

You may need to create a new community. The SISTERS Club is one such community. It is a space where you can come together with other like-minded women with a common goal of retirement success. It is the perfect forum to meet others like you and make new friends while securing your lives.

There are other ready-made communities, such as the service clubs. When I was active in Rotary, there was a widowed octogenarian gentleman who came to lunch meetings every week, and had done so for years. He was smart! He had a great community of friends with whom he could socialize and who cared enough about him to look out for him.

Another great place to develop a community is your place of worship. They are eager for members and go to great lengths to create a community environment with lots of fun activities.

Start developing your communities long before retirement. That will ease your transition out of the work environment. And when you do retire, you will be a well-established member of your new community.

Value Your Time with Meaningful Activities

Life is precious. Retirement is a golden opportunity—but for what? It's a big question, and one that's worth thinking about in advance. Sure, you'll want to take a vacation and maybe spend a few days at the beach, but then what?

I may be biased, but I think it is a wonderful time to create income from the hobbies you love. After all, you have the tools, you have the skills, and now you have the time. Make a commitment to yourself. It's also a perfect time to manage and continue to build your investment portfolio.

Retirement is a great time to be active. Don't waste it in passive activities, such as watching the world pass you by. Get interested. Be interesting. Be a participant in life.

Then find a way to give back. Giving creates its own meaning and starts its own chain reaction of life-fulfilling experiences. Volunteering is good for the heart. Charitable activities lead you down many fascinating paths that you will never experience if you don't get involved. And it has a way of creating its own loving community, just waiting for you.

Value Your Joy

There is an attractive brightness, a life-uplifting quality that emanates from those who understand the value of living life from a perspective of joy. *Joie de vivre* (literally, joy of living) is an irrepressible quality that creates its own good luck. If you don't experience joy in your life, look around for someone who does, and follow him or her around for a day. Don't go through life without joy. Joy comes from within and lights up the world. Let it shine. It is the most precious thing of all.

REFERENCES:

1 "Five Most Important Estate Planning Documents," and "Five Basic Estate Planning Documents," Wells Fargo Advisors.

AN INVITATION

THE JOURNEY DOESN'T STOP NOW—
IT'S ONLY JUST BEGINNING.

Find or start a SISTERS Club
using the resources at
www.sistersretirement.com

I invite you to contact me at
info@donnamphelan.com
or 800-375-2580
to continue the conversation.

I look forward to hearing from you.

BEST OF LUCK ON THE JOURNEY!

What Is a SISTERS Club?
(And Why You Need One!)

A group of women united with a cause can do anything. Look at Girl Scouts. Those moms are the most efficient, earth-moving, mountain-climbing, teen-motivating people on Earth. Who else would pack up four SUVs full of teenagers with camping supplies and take off for a weekend in the wilderness? And then repeat that exercise or a similar one, again and again, for years, forging characters in the process?

Look at what women have done for breast cancer research. Three decades ago, a handful of women met in the living room of Susan G. Komen's sister, Nancy Brinker. Susan had died from breast cancer. Before she died, Susan extracted a promise from her sister, Nancy, that she would do something about breast cancer. And so started the breast cancer research movement. Thirty years later, Susan G. Komen for the Cure™ has raised over $1 billion for breast cancer research. That's the power of women with a cause!

It is time now for women to rally to their own cause—retirement security. I predict this will be the number one economic issue facing senior women in the coming decades. Did you know that women in their eighties are the population group second most at risk, after children, of living in poverty?[1] Women deserve retirement peace of mind.

Women need to come together to combine their strengths and skills to generate income for retirement. Women need to create SISTERS: Several Stackable Income Streams To Empower Retirement Security. Women need to establish several income streams for retirement, because one income stream may dry up, like employment income or child support. Women need to band together to use all their moxie to protect themselves from hardship and create financial security in retirement.

How? By starting a SISTERS Club. A SISTERS Club is a group of women united together to support each other in creating retirement income security. It is like a bridge club or a book club, but instead of playing bridge or discussing books, women create small businesses to enrich their retirement. No matter how old you are, you are not too old to create retirement income. You will live twenty to forty years in retirement, and you will always need income.

When women come together in a club, they create hope, structure, and consistency. They share ideas and learn from each other. They discuss their successes and challenges, and help each other resolve problems.

Do you think you are incapable of starting a small business? Think again! Mrs. Fields started a cookie company. Mary Kay Ash started a cosmetics company. Muriel Siebert started an investment company. Martha Stewart started a catering company. What are your skills? What are your interests?

A small business does not have to be sophisticated. But it does have to be smart. Above all, it must generate income. Women underestimate themselves and their abilities. They downplay the number of high-level skills they already have just to manage a family—planner, purchaser, budgeter, scheduler, negotiator, transportation manager, menu preparer, organizer—in short, CEO!

Why should you start a SISTERS Club? Because if you are like the average woman, you will need more income for retirement. You have worked a lifetime earning far less than your male counterparts. You have spent your time and money taking care of kids and aging parents. Like most women, you have put yourself last in order of priority. Consequently, you have much less in savings than you will need to get you through retirement. It is imperative that you *start now* to create a SISTERS Club to figure out how to create income for retirement.

A SISTERS Club creates an environment where women can join together and brainstorm. Women can combine their talents to create income-generating business ventures—either individually or as a group. They can pool their skills and resources to complement and augment each other's abilities. Perhaps one woman has marketing skills, another is good at strategy, a third has good accounting abilities, and yet another has an idea or prototype for a product.

Women must think out of the box in order to thrive in retirement. For example, most retired women live alone and pay all their own household expenses. Often, they have very little left over for retirement savings or to put into a business venture. What if women were to engage in residence sharing? That would give them as much as 50 percent more every month to put into income-generating vehicles, such as dividend-paying stocks or a small business.

What do you need to start a SISTERS Club? You need a place to meet, a few friends, a pad of paper, and an idea. And perseverance. Pick those friends with whom you are compatible, and who share your work ethic and enthusiasm. Then go to www.sistersretirement.com and register your SISTERS Club. There you will find resources to help you learn how to start a SIS-TERS Club. You will learn how to start a business and can download templates for writing a business plan. You will also find a "Share Your Story" tab, where you can share your successes.

By creating collaborative economic teams for financial success, women can successfully create income streams that will support them well throughout retirement. Women need to step up now and take responsibility for their own retirement. Most women will not get pensions, and Social Security is not enough to live on. Give yourself the gift of financial security in your senior years.

It's up to you. Take the challenge now. Start a SIS-TERS Club—no matter how old you are. Have fun with it. Secure yourself for retirement. No one else will do it for you. And no one else will live your retirement lifestyle for you. Create SISTERS—Several Stackable Income Streams To Empower Retirement Security. You will need several income streams for retirement. Join with other women to create the great lifestyles you want, made possible by the income streams you create. Together we are stronger. Women with a cause can do anything. Make that cause your retirement security.

REFERENCES:

1 US Census.

How to Start a SISTERS Club

1. *SISTERS Club Structure*
    Each club must start with a minimum of two
    members. There is no maximum number of
    members. The first order of business is to choose
    a club name. This may include the club location,
    product, slogan, or any other appropriate name.

2. *Registration of SISTERS Clubs*
    SISTERS Clubs should register their club at
    SISTERSretirement.com. SISTERS Clubs are
    encouraged to update their membership, keep an
    online diary of progress, and share success stories
    at this site.

3. *Purpose of SISTERS Clubs*
    The purpose of the SISTERS Club is to create an
    environment where women can come together to

share knowledge and experiences, generate ideas, and create investments and business ventures that will provide on-going retirement income for the members of the Club. It is a community of women helping women and helping themselves to improve their retirement planning success.

4. *Individually Owned Business (IOB)*
The members may create individually owned businesses (IOB). In that case, each member would create and control her own business. The members would come together to share their experiences, offering each other advice, professional contacts, and moral support.

5. *Club-Owned Business (COB)*
The club may decide to create a club-owned business (COB). In this case, the club will create and record member shares. Each member automatically gets one share, the assumption being that each person will bring some human value other than monetary. Thereafter, each share is purchased for $1,000, or in fractions or multiples thereof, and approved by majority vote. All profits are reinvested back into the business for the first three years. Thereafter, profits, above and beyond operating needs, as approved by majority vote, are distributed according to the number of shares each person holds.

6. *Club Member Commitment*

   All club members agree to meet regularly and must commit for one year. The club will choose a regular meeting place or rotate between members' homes.

7. *Define Member Roles*
   a. Club leader—sets agenda. Keeps meeting productive and friendly. Helps establish goals and measure results.
   b. Secretary—keeps track of meeting minutes, votes, and initiatives.
   c. Treasurer—keeps track of money, bank statements.

   Members should switch roles every six to twelve months, as agreed upon by the members.

8. *Contractual Arrangement of Fairness (CAF)*

   All members of a club-owned business must sign a contractual arrangement of fairness (CAF). An attorney should be consulted to vet the legality and fairness of the document.

9. *Terms of Agreement*

   All SISTERS Club members must agree to the terms of agreement found at SISTERSretirement.com, which includes, confidentiality, trust and mutual respect.

10. *Mastermind Team of Advisors*

It is recommended that every SISTERS Club enlist a team of advisors to establish and help manage their businesses. These include the following:

a. CPA

b. Attorney

c. Financial advisor

d. Bank

e. Insurance specialist

As the business grows, it may be necessary to enlist additional specialists.

11. *Club Strengths and Interests*

Define your club's interests, strengths, and skills. This will help you recognize natural abilities of individual members that can be best used to create a business. It will also point to the most suitable product or service for your club's skill set.

12. *Club Business, Product, or Service*

Define your club's product or service. Try to define it in depth. For example, if you decide to start a T-shirt company, define what kind of T-shirts you want to sell and to whom. Who will design and produce the T-shirts. Why would someone buy your T-shirts? Where will you sell your T-shirts? How will you deliver them? How much will you charge for them?

The more you can define your product or service the better you can market it.

Consider carefully any hobbies your club members may have. Hobbies hold tremendous potential because it is something that you or one of your members already loves and understands. Chances are, she already knows how to make a product and has the tools and supplies to do so. Can the other members rally round this product? Can you transform it from a hobby into a viable business?

You and/or your club may decide that you want to have a service-based business. If you are good at cooking, you could start a catering company. If you have good bookkeeping skills, you could start a bookkeeping company. If you have a green thumb, you could start a gardening company, and make an arrangement with the local nursery to service its customers.

13. *Business Strategy*

Define your business strategy. Strategy means "how." How will you make your business a success? Will you sell your product on the Internet? How will you generate interest? Will you compete on price? Will you sell unique artistic products available only through your business? How will you beat out the competition and make your business a success?

14. *Marketing Plan*

Create a marketing plan to sell your product or service. How will you get the word out about your fantastic product?

15. *Define Your Timeline*

Set business goals. Be specific and measure your results.

16. *Business Plan*

Every legitimate business has a formal business plan. Take your business seriously and write a business plan. It should include the six "Ps":

- People—whom will you sell to, hire, and interact with?
- Product—what product or service will you offer?
- Place—where will you sell your product or service; also, where will you locate your business?
- Price—how will you price your product, what pricing policy will you establish?
- Promotion—how will you promote your project?
- Projections—these are financial projections of how much money you expect to earn in one, three, and five years; you should also include an approximation of costs.

17. *How to Finance Your Venture*

Get creative. Start small. Sell one T-shirt, use the profits to buy two more. Sell two T-shirts, use the profits to buy three more, and so on. By starting small and reinvesting your profits back into your business, you will be able to finance your business out of your own pocket.

Club-owned businesses may agree to each invest a small amount as a start-up in the business. Just be sure that you have a contractual arrangement of fairness signed by all members first.

18. *Do Not Incur Debt*

Since your business is specifically to generate income for retirement, it is critically important that you do not go into debt to finance your business.

19. *Business Analysis*

Analyze your business successes and challenges. Repeat your successes. Look for creative solutions to your challenges.

20. *New Members*

New members should be sponsored by a current club member and approved by a majority vote. New members are encouraged to visit the club to ensure compatibility.

21. *Resolving Disputes*

Disputes should be handled in an open and fair manner by the entire club in a way that reduces discord among the members.

22. *Member Termination*

Members who wish to resign from a club should do so in writing. If the club wishes to terminate a member, it must be approved by a majority vote. The treasurer should ensure that the terminating member is brought current on account if she is a shareholder.

23. *Dissolution of a Club*

Clubs may be dissolved by a majority vote of the members. The treasurer should ensure that all financial obligations are finalized and accounts closed.

INDEX

CPSIA information can be obtained at www.ICGtesting.com
Printed in the USA
BVOW09*2113011214

376268BV00003BA/3/P